My Autobiography

At the age of Eighty-Six, after many years of thought and now four grandchildren, this is my story.

Part One

Where It All Started

I was born on 31st May 1932 on the Island of Rousay at Westness Farm to my parents, both Orcadians. Mum was from Kirkwall and Dad from Lyness on the Island of Hoy. Mum was housekeeper to the Minister on the Island and Dad was farming Lyness Farm with his parents, my Grandfather who was born on Fara – now uninhabited.

When the German Fleet was getting lifted at the end of the 1914-1918 war, Granddad went on the crane to do this as it was better pay than he could earn for Dad and him on the farm. So, Mum used to come over from the manse to collect the milk for them and Dad, and she started courting. Dad was mainly working the farm solely. They got married on 8th July 1931 in St Magnus Cathedral, stayed in a hut on the farm for a little while then moved to Westness Farm, and later to Dounby on the mainland where my brother was born.

After a few years, they moved down south to a farm in Midlothian near Penicuik, where my second brother was born. I started school at Nine Mile Burn, was there for one year then moved to East Lothian where Dad became Grieve on a farm in the Morham area.

I started at Morham School aged six and continued there with a wonderful teacher called Mrs McKenzie. I enjoyed school, sat my qualifying examination there and came 1st place with qualifications which took me to Knox Academy in a Grade A class. Mrs McKenzie took a great interest in me and would ask me to stay overnight on many occasions in the School House in order to help me with homework, etc. She took a great interest in me on my way forward at the Knox Academy. However, when I came of age to leave school at fourteen, I wanted to leave and work in a shop, an ambition to serve people, much to my parents' disappointment and Mrs McKenzie's.

My Grandparents had also left Orkney and were living in Edinburgh by now. I loved my Grandparents and spent much of my school holidays with them. Their daughter, my Aunt Violet, was nine years older than me, and living and working from home. She was like a sister to me. She took me to all the exciting places in Edinburgh and made lovely clothes for me, herself and Granny, so I decided I was going to stay with them, working in a shop. That would not be possible at Morham as there was only a bus on a Saturday to Haddington. It was worked out I would stay in Edinburgh. I felt I was really stepping out.

A new Draper Shop was opening a branch on Easter Road called Sparks. I was interviewed with Granny asking Mr

Sparks all the necessary questions. She was excellent at that. I got started and enjoyed serving the public. After a year, Mum and Dad moved to a farm near Gladsmuir in East Lothian. I thought 'I think I would like to go home now and look for a job in Haddington'. I had some experience now and saw an advert for an assistant in a drapers in Haddington called Bells, not realising when I went for the interview that Mr Bell was Mr Sparks' brother-in-law. I again got the job at twenty-one shillings a week, two shillings more than in Sparks. I learned such a lot with Tom Bell and his son Bertie. There was a Gents' Department, middle shop, materials, wool, clothes for children, and a Ladies Shop – three departments with their own doors on to the street. I was in the middle one and helping in Gents on Saturdays when it was extra busy.

The Ukrainians were getting demobbed and coming in for suits, hats, shirts etc. for which I had to measure and help them to choose. I did not mind doing the chest, head, neck etc. but I was embarrassed on the trouser bit – inside leg. However, I really liked the shop work and got promoted to be head girl, pricing the articles when they came in. They had a code on them, for example, N/T was 2/3. I learned it all as this code was the price Bells paid for the stock - so the code was at top of the ticket I affixed to each garment and the price that it was to sell at was below. I was the only member of staff that got the code and I used this till the time for stocktaking.

The farmers' wives all used to come into Haddington on a Friday as their husbands were at the Corn Exchange with their produce and samples. Mr Bell would go through to the Ladies Department and talk to them and then come through to the middle department.

One day he said to me 'When I take them through, I say to them come through here and I will show you the best girl I have ever had to work for me.' Great praise to get, but I loved the job. They taught me window dressing and I always had to cut the curtain net material as the other girls used to run off the straight and waste a lot. The answer was to look at the point of your scissors and keep them straight. The business, more or less, next door was a Grocers and the girl who worked in there came into Bells and said to me 'Mr McDonald would like you to come and see him when you finish tonight.' I went in and he said he was offering me a job to come and work for him and his brother, mainly to do the book-keeping and send out accounts but, again, on Friday and Saturday afternoons to go on to the counter. I thought this looked good – a high stool and desk for the account job and then the counter work. I put my notice in to Bells and Tom Bell said, 'I saw that girl talking to you'. He had his office at the bottom of the department I worked in and he would open the door and watch what was going on. I was again getting offered more money. He was completely annoyed and went to see Mr McDonald and accused him of poaching his staff.

After a discussion I did go to McDonalds and what sticks in my mind was on a busy Friday afternoon I was on the counter cutting a big cheese with a wire and serving next to Ian McDonald. We had a queue. There was an Irishman who worked on one of the farms next in the queue with this rather demanding posh lady, who always wanted Ian to give her the best of attention, standing behind the Irishman. When it was his turn the lady stepped forward in front of him as if to say he is of no account and I want you to serve me and Ian said to her 'Excuse me, this gentleman is before you' and asked the Irishman 'What would you like sir?' I always remember that, well done, Ian! After about one and a half years, Mr Bell approached me again to see if I would come back and I did! Six months after that, Mr McDonald came to the house to see if I would come back to him, but I stayed where I was this time.

We were now living at Beanston Farm. I met my first boyfriend, then the Grieve's son, who worked in the Courier office. We attended the Athelstaneford dances. I thought that there could never be anyone else in the world like this boy (first love). However, the time came when he had to go and do his National Service. I thought it was the end of the world. He came home on leave a few times. He was in the Royal Signals. Then he was sent off to Egypt for the rest of the time and I used to come home looking at the mantelpiece for an airmail letter with all the endearing words on it. Then, you could send a special song to be played for them via some organisation, so I sent 'Yours till the stars lose the glory', etc.

I got used to going to the dances without a boyfriend and I loved this as I lived for the dances. I had about another four girl pals and thought it was much more fun not sitting with a boyfriend - you did not get asked by others very much. Now I was getting loads of dances and I was dancing three nights a week, usually Athelstaneford on Fridays, great bands always played in the Corn Exchange in Haddington every Saturday - I adored that and the Catholic Hall on a Wednesday with Chrissie Bathgate playing. She was a good friend as she was Clerkess in Bells and I used to go home with her at lunch times. Her mum was a great cook.

Her dad worked in the Killing House over at the Nungate so plenty of good beef, etc. Chrissie sometimes played at Westruther and a bus would go. I went also and her dad, who liked a good drink and was mostly drunk. She would say to me 'Don't tell anyone that he is my dad.' I also attended a lot of barn dances on the various farms starting at 7.00pm finishing at 4.00am. Having dances was great fun.

There was a boy from the Drem Small Holdings who worked with his dad. They had it mainly as dairy farming. He used to give me the odd dance and chat - he did know that I had a boyfriend with me at that time. (This was before he went off to National Service). It was mostly at the Athelstaneford dances, but my favourite place was the Corn Exchange. I did not want a boyfriend. I just wanted to dance as many dances as possible. I looked for good dancers - my pals were looking for boyfriends. I was often asked if they could take me to the pictures in Haddington on a particular night. I always said 'OK' I did not seem to be able to say 'no'. I knew fine I would not be at the pictures when the dancing was available. There were many boys who I knew would be standing outside the picture house waiting on me. The strange thing was they never ever tackled me about it. They just felt you had stood them up in those days. Nowadays, they would really sort you out.

The boy from the holdings now had a girlfriend with him at the dances but would still give me a dance. He knew I went to the Corn Exchange and he would say 'If I am on my own on a Saturday night in Haddington, I will come there'. I could see he was wanting to get out of his present situation. One Friday night, he asked, 'Will you be at

Athelstaneford next Friday?' and I said I would. Of course, I never gave it another thought as there was a dance in the Corn Exchange on that night. I only learned that during the week so of course my pals and I decided on the Corn Exchange. After an hour or so at the Corn Exchange, I went through to the toilet and there was this fellow and his pals at the bar. He said immediately 'You are supposed to be at Athelstaneford.' I said, 'So are you!' 'We are going down on the North Berwick bus at 11 o'clock', so he came through. I had got paid in by another boy who I had given-in to and gone to the pictures with during the week – one of my brother's pals - so he and the small holder and another two and were all hanging around where I was. So, they latterly decided it was bus time and Duncan from the holdings asked if I would go to the pictures with him on Saturday night. I said 'Yes', and I knew this time I was going to go. The wink I got when I was dancing with someone else won me over. Hence, I did meet him and go to the pictures and that was my new boyfriend. A 'Dear John' letter was written to the boy serving in Egypt. I no longer gave the song 'Yours' another thought. This was it.

After a few months, Dad decided he was going to leave Beanston and move as Grieve to a farm near Kirkliston. I no way wanted to go. I was not moving away from Duncan so what now? I will have to get a job where I can live in and work. I went to Roodlands Hospital as a Kitchen Maid for a few months but knew this was a stop-gap. I was looking for somewhere else. I learned quite a bit of cooking as I was assistant to the Cook at Roodlands. Then I saw they were looking for a Cook at Fenton Barns. I applied to the farmhouse there, got the job, solely cooking and baking for the family and endless visitors. I had good accommodation, a bedroom and a separate sitting room. I gained a lot more experience there and it was near for Duncan to cycle down and see me.

After about six months, when Dad and Mum moved to the Kirkliston area, it was Christmas and Duncan asked me to get engaged so I spoke it over with Dad and told him he would be getting asked by Duncan and did he have any objections? I was very close to Dad and he to me, and he asked 'what if I say no?' and I said 'well it won't matter'. 'Well,' he said, 'what is the point of asking?' 'Well, Dad, the point is if you say no I will say no' and I truly meant it as I always listened to what he said. However, he did say yes to Duncan and we got engaged and had a get-together at their house at Kirkliston. Then after that Dad moved back again to East Lothian this time near to Gifford, Howden Farm. I then felt I wanted to go and live near them again.

I saw in the paper that Lady Tweedale of Yester House was looking for a Lady's Maid. I applied and got the job. I lived in but was a ten-minute bus run from home. My duties were to look after her personally, lay out her clothes for each occasion and that included every night for dinner, plus she had her own family and the Lord had his own family who visited regularly. He had daughters who had titles of Lady. I had to attend to them and choose from their luggage what they would wear for dinner. They kept the tradition that who was on Lord Tweedale's arm would be the most important lady visitor and her husband would be with Lady Tweedale. All others paired with a partner and followed en route to the dining room led by the Lord and they entered two by two.

I did my morning work and then changed into my black dress for afternoon and evening (if I had to work) but usually I was finished after they departed for dinner. I was head of the other servants when we ate in the servants' hall - very sparse with food - I was down to eight stone – I was normally nine and half stone. I used to pop along to Mum's for something to eat if I got an hour or so off during the day. Again, I felt I needed to move after approximately two years. I looked for somewhere nearer to Drem. Lochhill between Drem and Longniddry was looking for a cook-come-nanny. I applied and again I was successful.

Lady Tweedale was very disappointed when I gave notice. She asked 'Are you getting married?' 'Not for another year' I replied. 'Well, you have been a wonderful member of staff. Please let me know when your marriage date is fixed, and I want to give you your bouquet of flowers and for your bridesmaid and your two flower girls.' She loved her garden and did make floral arrangements. One of the reasons I left was because I used to get embarrassed in the servants' hall when the Butlers and Maids came to stay like the Duke of Sutherland for example. The food was so scarce and skimpy like a quarter slice of bread with some bacon on it for tea. We got two digestive biscuits on Tuesdays. What a treat! I told Lady Tweedale how I felt. She said she would see to it, but it never altered. I don't know if she spoke to the Cook or if the Cook had her reason for saving the food.

I had a lovely job at Lochhill and was treated as a member of the family - two lovely little girls. I did all the cooking. My date for marriage was arranged for October 30th, 1954. When I announced this, I was told another baby was on the way and due in mid-November. I did not want to change the date as my future Father and Mother-in-law were moving out of the small holding in early November. I did get married on 30th October in Bolton Church and the reception was held in the Black Bull, Haddington.

We had a lovely day and left from there to go to the Station Hotel in Perth, overnight by train and then get the train at Perth Station in the morning to have a week in Inverness. We had a lovely time and realised a whole new life lay ahead of us now. My Father-in-law decided he was leaving three weeks later to coincide with their move to Ballencrieff to start with. Duncan's brother had a small holding in Drem also, so we stayed there.

After one week I met my old boss coming up the Drem road in his car. He said his wife was to rest up as she had high blood pressure, and could I possibly come back until the baby arrived as the girl who took over from me was pretty useless. He said 'Duncan can come and stay also.

You can have the guest room' so this is what we did. The poor girl was crying off and on and told me she had no confidence as she was getting told all the time 'May did it this way or that way'. I could understand what she meant. I tried to help her as I was doing the cooking and looking after the children and she did the housework. Girl number three arrived after a week and I stayed on until mum was up and about and getting into a routine. I was glad I had managed to do this as they had been so good to me and they always visited me and kept in touch after I moved into Drem. The girls did too into their teens.

Part Two

Small Holder's Wife – a complete change now

My brother-in-law and ourselves, plus my father-in-law, travelled from Ballencrieff daily and all worked together although the largest holding, forty acres, had been signed over by the Department of Agriculture to Duncan on his father's retirement. At this stage I did not do anything outside, probably an odd time at the potato riddle and looking after the hens as there were three men doing the work on the two holdings. It was a dairy farm we had so Duncan did all the milking with the machines himself at 8.00am in the morning and 6.00pm in the evening. The milk went to the Scottish Milk Marketing Board. We got paid monthly by cheque from Glasgow on 24th of every month. I got £24 and my sister-in-law got £24 to keep the house with food. I was having the three men for 10 o'clock tea in the morning, my father-in-law and Duncan for lunch every day.

I was struggling. I had never been as hard up in all my life as I was then. I had seen my mother-in-law live very sparsely and I could not understand it. Now I thought I do. This is almost impossible. Seeing it with new eyes, you see things differently. Father-in-law was very much acting the boss and criticising anything we did. The hens were messing on top of the hay, so Duncan and I decided there was a corrugated shed opposite the hay shed, with no front on it so that evening the two of us put netting on the front and decided we would keep the hens in there.

The following morning, Father-in-law questioned me on who did that. I said 'Duncan and I'. 'He is useless', he replied. I could not take that. My reply was 'if you are here, I do not see the point of us being here'. No one ever spoke to him in the negative. He was king of the manor. At 5.00pm he explained to Duncan he would not be back. We had been given eight cows and the implements when we took over as Duncan had worked for ten shillings pocket money for ten years.

Within a few days a lawyer's letter arrived claiming the cows plus the implements he had left. When I defended this at a meeting in the house, he was told if you claim one son you must claim the other also, as it is a Partnership. The Partnership was dissolved, and we were now completely on our own.

For the first time I could now put things in place the way I could see it. Instead of three men working, everything was our own, thirty-eight acres and dairy cows were in our hands with one daughter aged two. Now needing to help with everything that was happening outside, it was hard going but my determination when I knew I could make a difference here kept me going. We also bought two sows and thought breeding some pigs would be another source of income. I was also pregnant with our second child but kept working until, not surprising, I had to be taken into the Vert Hospital with high blood pressure one week early. Anne, my daughter, went to my Mum and Dad's while I was in hospital. Seven days before the birth was due I had a second daughter Fiona and had to stay another ten days. I was away from home for seventeen days. Duncan struggled on his own with rain, snow, etc.

Early in April, the day I came home, there was a huge wooden tea chest in front of the Raeburn in the kitchen with young piglets in it. The sow had farrowed the night before. The weather was horrendous. The sow was in a shed where obviously there was so much water from melting snow, etc that it had got flooded. Duncan was obviously so exhausted doing the dairy and pigs and visiting me, he had not got up during the night to check; something I always did with the cows as well. He was so concerned trying to save the piglets he hardly noticed I had arrived with our new daughter. Mum and Dad were there. Mum had a nice fire on. Dad picked me up from hospital and was helping Duncan.

Now back into harness as it was for me, I had to go out and help wash milk pails and dishes with water heated by steam. You lit a fire then waited for the steam to blow off into a tub of cold water and get them into the steamer. When you were ready to go out and do this, the steam had not blown off and when it did, no matter what you were doing, you had to get there. It was an essential part of everyday cleanliness for the Milk Marketing Board that lifted the milk in ten-gallon cans after the milk had been put through the cooler each morning and evening. This was our main source of income, plus help with the feeding of cows in the byre etc.

By this time Fiona, who was a very difficult infant, hardly ever slept at night and was difficult most of the day. By the time she reached eight months I was totally exhausted, feeling sick most of the time. I said to Duncan 'I can't continue at this pace. We will need to get a young boy to come and work. I don't mind him staying in the house with us as long as I don't have to go outside'. We were lucky enough to hear of a lad from Maysheil near Gifford who was looking for a job, who was around sixteen or seventeen years of age. Duncan interviewed him, and Pat arrived, very willing and hard working. I began to pick up. Patrick stayed for about two years. The children were getting older and I could help again.

My Mum and Dad had a small holding at Letham Mains near Haddington and they were going off for a holiday up north. Dad had a van – no car - as he had a round where he delivered eggs and potatoes. I asked Duncan 'why do we not offer them our Ford Consul car and we could have the van? It would be more comfortable for them in the car'. This was arranged.

They had just gone off and we were walking down the field to see how the turnips were growing which was feed for the cows. Duncan said 'I am surprised they are so far on. They are already the size of shopping turnips.' A light flashed in my mind as I used to see some of the small holdings taking vegetables to the market in Edinburgh. So, I drove off in the van to Edinburgh market where all the different traders were, Clarkes, Veitch Moir, etc. I asked if I could have turnip nets and showed them a sample. They said bring thirty nets tomorrow morning. I was back home helping Duncan to get them ready. He loaded the van. I went off at 5.30am. Duncan did not milk until 8.00am so I knew I could be back in time to see the children. Then at 11.00am that morning, I got a phone call. "Can you bring the same tomorrow and every day?" They wanted the same. I did this for the two weeks when Mum and Dad were away.

On the Friday I thought that would be it as Dad was coming back on the Saturday and I knew he would need his van. On the Friday morning when I was at the market, they asked 'the same on Monday Mrs. Fairbairn?' I replied okay. Driving home I thought now what? Then I had a thought. If I could buy a trailer for the car I could continue. How am I going to do this before Monday morning?

When I got home, The Courier had been delivered to us. I opened it and a Trailer for Sale advert was there. The chap, Cockburn had been building a butcher's shop for himself and he had finished it (now Stirling & Burnet). I went up and bought it – told him I could not take it home until the weekend. I crossed the road to Roses Garage and asked if I could get a tow bar on my car, but it would need to be Sunday as I was not getting the car until Saturday evening. They agreed. I had the tow bar and the trailer home, turnips loaded for Monday morning.

I could not reverse a trailer and still can't but that did not hold me back as the market was in a circle - you could drive right round all the various stalls. So if there were no spaces as it was very busy with shop-keepers picking up and growers dropping off, I had to keep driving round until I got a space. I thought we could grow some cabbages, spring onions, cauliflowers, etc, which I managed to commence. Duncan and I kept going. We had regular cheques coming in now and not depending on the one milk cheque on 24th of every month.

I got more ambitious and thought on my way home, in the morning I would stop at Musselburgh and ask the fruit and vegetable shops if they wanted any, and I had three shops in Musselburgh and I then went to Port Seton and Prestonpans on the way home so that was cash for me. They started asking for potatoes. I could not handle the potatoes, so we bought a larger van and Duncan had to deliver the potatoes and other vegetables to them, but he never went to the market as we still had the cows and milking had to be done. So I did not need to go to the market.

I still wanted to make money. Those hard-up days, I was determined, were behind me. I was going to make a better life for the four of us I decided. By now the girls were both at school, so I said to Duncan 'I am going to apply for a job with Market Research'. They were looking for Interviewers for East Lothian and the Borders. Duncan said 'You are not doing that. No small holder's wife in this scheme goes out to work except for the holding'. I said 'Well, this will be the first one. Just watch'.

I applied, and I got the job. It was when coffee granules were being researched. I had to get a cross-section of people of different work status and age groups, leave a sample, call back and get their opinion. I had an Austin Westminster car. It was great and very comfortable. It was a very cold job as it was winter, and I bought a suede coat, gloves and hat from Main Saddlers and off I went. When I did the Borders, I would do hundred miles if I was working in Coldstream, there and back. It worked out okay as Duncan was always there for the girls coming home if I wasn't back.

I also used to be asked to come and teach at Athelstaneford School if the Infant Mistress was off sick, so I got quite good experience. They told Mr Meiklejohn, Education Officer, that they wanted me, and he looked back at my school records and recommended that I could do this as an uncertified teacher at fifteen shillings a day at that time. I then saw that the Compass Private School in Haddington was looking for an Infant Teacher for mornings, 9.00am – 12.30pm. I applied and, with the reference from Athelstaneford, I got that post. I worked both that and the research job for a bit then gave up Market Research but kept on at Compass School. It was the happiest I had ever been in any job. I absolutely adored it. We had the long summer holidays as well as Easter and Christmas and no weekend work.

One day at Compass School, Mrs Younger, Principal and Founder of the school, approached Mary, the teacher who I passed my class on to each year and asked us, or more or less told us, she had entered us to do a weekend course on Modern Maths at the "Corpus Christie College" in Cambridge. It was suggested by her that we could travel by train, but I offered to drive down with my Austin Westminster overdrive car. Looking back that was a huge undertaking. I did not think of that at all then. I had great self-belief and confidence in myself. I had tackled much bigger challenges.

I picked up Mary on the Friday morning outside her home, the 'Tyneside Tavern' in Haddington at 8.00am. No Sat Navs or motorways then. Mary had the map and did the navigation. We arrived in Cambridge latish in the afternoon and were absolutely very hungry. I pulled in immediately at the first restaurant, an Indian one. As I entered, it looked so drab, curtains hanging around and very dismal. Normally I would never have sat down but a seat and something to eat and relax was definitely an essential. We now had to find the College which did not seem a problem. We booked in and as it was College holiday time, we were allocated student rooms next door to each other.

Our first class and introduction were on Friday evening and went well. Glad to go to bed and had to be at class for 9.00am on Saturday morning. Again, very informative.

Stopped for lunch and another class at 2.00pm and then 6.00pm, finishing at 8.00pm. Mary was of Catholic faith and was very anxious to know where she could go for Mass on Sunday morning. As we entered the evening class there were two nuns in the class, so she was very relieved when she saw them and immediately asked them where she could go. They explained it was more or less across the road and approx. hundred yards. We decided once the class finished we would go and see where it was. Mary put on her headscarf and went in. I waited outside, and she felt more relaxed now.

At 8.15am on Sunday morning, a knock at my door. It was Mary and I asked 'Oh, are you going to Mass?' I was still in my nightwear. I was going to get up at 8.30am. Mary said 'No, I have already been. We shall go for breakfast now'. Another class followed and after lunch, we were taken by bus to another part of the course.

Then Monday was the test day. Do we go home with a Pass Certificate or not? Fortunately, we both passed. So glad we both did, as it would have been awful for one to pass and one not. It would have been a difficult journey home and more difficult to report back to school.

Mrs Younger was very pleased to see we had been successful as it was good for the school's profile. The journey home went very well. We were both glad to be in East Lothian again.

Coming near to summer holidays one year, after having been there by this time for almost three years, I was round in the hay shed helping Duncan and this chap, who used to come and help him if he was really busy off and on and also used to help with the horses down at Gullane owned by a Sir - a bit of a character - who had a personal horse called Araby. He used to ride it to the Castle Hotel at Dirleton and get drunk. The horse was tied up outside. Then he would more or less just lie across it and it would take him home.

He had some not very honest people taking the horses on the beach and making a lot of money during the summer. However, he was in a bad way financially and this chap used to go with him in a lovely trap and Araby and come up past our holdings and stop at the gate. He was dressed like a cowboy.

The day I am referring to, he had asked this fellow to come up and see us as he was getting all his horses lifted for debt, but he did not want to lose his Araby. Would we take the horse and hide it for a week until the creditors had lifted the riding horses? I was not keen as I thought that was a bit deceptive, but Duncan said we would keep it at the back of the hay shed. After a few days the chap came back and said 'He is wondering if you would like to buy the horse' and I said 'No. What would we do with a horse?' Duncan said 'I would like a horse.' He had worked with them before the tractor. 'Okay. If you want a horse, we will get it.' The girls already had ponies by this time and two days later he was back. 'Do you want to buy the trap?' 'No' again I said. Duncan said 'I would like the trap'. 'What are you going to do with it?' I asked. 'I'll go up the road with Araby and the trap'. I replied 'you will never do that in front of the neighbours'. 'I will'. Okay we will buy the trap' and next was the harness.

By the time I got down for that, the cowboy was on the wall waiting for me and the money. Needless to say, the horse and the trap were doing nothing. I had another thought. If I could get a licence to go on to North Berwick beach with the horse and trap at the height of the holiday season and if it coincided with my long holidays at Compass, I could give that a go. I never ever told anyone when I had made my plan, not even Duncan, until I was ready and had it started as I always thought if you discuss your plans, they will talk about the obstacles. I went up to the County Buildings and got my licence.

Now Duncan agreed to get a horse trailer built to get the horse up and down. Also, I had to learn how to put the harness on and attach it from the horse to the gig. This was done by my Dad. He had done quite a bit with horses and also breaking-in Shetland ponies, and loading them on the boat, with them climbing the sides, when he farmed in Orkney. I had never done anything with horses apart from the two girls having their ponies with which Dad also helped. However, my determination was as strong as ever and my belief that if you have the confidence in yourself and faith, it can get you there. I had arranged for the trailer to be built - that was the horse transport bit done - now the gig. It needed to stay at North Berwick - I could not take that up and down daily. So, I approached the Bass Rock Garage and asked if I could possibly keep it there. They agreed. I decided to start on a Saturday as it was holiday time - school holidays, people staying in North Berwick from all over.

I loaded the horse and set off - the gig was already down there. I still could not reverse our trailer, so I drove into the station car park and unloaded the horse, led it down the brae to the garage. The men there were so helpful, they pulled the gig out and showed me how to fix it up and off I went along past the putting green and then down onto the beach.

I had a notice with me to put up and in no time, I had a queue. I could manage to take six at a time if they were of average build or some children. I stood at the front and drove the gig along my chosen distances. I did around two and a half hours on my first day to see how it went. I was pleased by the result. Back to the garage, loosen off the gig, up the hill, load up and make for home with my leather money bag that went over my shoulder, like a bus conductor. Dad had given it to me as he had used it for his egg and potato round at one time. I drove in the gate and had just got round to start to unload the horse when Mum and Dad drove in. Unknown to me they had obviously been concerned about what I was doing and so they had driven from Letham Holdings down to North Berwick and sat on the grass that sloped up from the beach and watched me in case anything went wrong - Dad would be there to help. They had watched me load up without being seen at the station, given me a bit of a start and followed me. I was overwhelmed by their concern and their dedication to watch over me. Real love! I continued to do this daily as it was the summer season and I had the long holidays from Compass School.

I then was asked a few times at the beach if they could sit on the horse and of course I said no, but it got my mind going again. I thought if I could get them to come up to the holding, I could use the horse plus the girls' ponies to give them a ride. It was hard work doing what I was doing, travelling every day. Sometimes, if the sprinkler was on at the putting green, the horse would take off, but he always stopped and went down quite quietly at his usual bit. I sometimes thought I would end up at the bottom of the High Street. I also felt the rubber on the edges of the tyres of the gig were getting worn with the turning. I had found it very viable and profitable, however I made up my mind to try the rides from the holding – much to the girls' disapproval as they did not want anyone on their ponies.

It did work so well I had to keep getting another horse and another one and so on. We used to hack them out up the road along the top of a field which took us to Athelstaneford and down a path at the end of the village which took us back down the road – which took an hour to ride. We did this – we being me and the two girls. I had to adapt myself to ride now with one daughter at the front of the ride and the younger daughter, a born natural on a pony, in the middle so she could go back and forward to help anyone who was letting their horse's head go down and go along the grass like a lawnmower, and me at the back so I could see all that was going on. This became a great success. We did this after school into the evening and all day at weekends and every day at the holidays.

The girls never had time to play during holidays. They worked all the time and I had to get some good riders to come and help during the holidays. I was still at Compass and a lot of my custom came from there. My plan was that I would just do this until the girls left school. However, Anne, my elder daughter was now coming up for sixteen. She had worked with me since she was twelve and was very clever at school.

She announced to me as it was nearing the time for school holidays again that she wanted to make a career out of horses, so she would stay at home. I said 'definitely not, you are not going to spend your life doing this. I am not objecting to you working with horses, but you must go away and train and sit your exams and get qualified in an equestrian career and then you can come back home, and we will upgrade our own business.'

I wanted the best training place for her. We had an Irish ex-jockey who used to come down and ride. He was a school janitor and since he married, we became very friendly and he said to me there was a top training yard in Dublin. 'You don't want her too near home as the training is hard and she would come back home'. I approached Iris Kellet who had trained a lot of top-class riders, Eddie Macken for one, who was well known in the show jumping world and was on television many times and was there when Anne was accepted, after her and I flew over to Dublin and had an interview. Iris was very choosy who she took. She would only have one person from each different country. She never wanted another one from the same one. She obviously had her own ideas about that. There were American, South African, Canadian, French and Anne from Scotland.

She went off in June when the school holidays started, was quite homesick at first and I missed her terribly. I was left with Fiona, my younger daughter and I thought what now? How can we manage? Life takes amazing turns.

I was on the Management Committee of Typnepark School and the staff knew I ran a riding school as well. One day, one of the senior staff members came to see me and said they had taken the girls pony trekking at Stenton and one girl was a natural. Would I be prepared to let her have a day at the riding school helping? I agreed. I also could see she was a natural. I told her she could come as often as she wanted. She came by bus. I was told she was aggressive, a thief, etc. I found in my eyes she was no problem. She found a £1 note in the field, brought it to me and said someone must have lost this out of their pocket when they were riding. I thought <u>honesty</u> is the word for this. I got a telephone call one day from Tynepark saying as she had played havoc the night before and she was going up in front of a Panel in Edinburgh the following day and the outcome would likely be Borstal. I asked 'is there anything I can do?' as I was very fond of her by now and wanted to take her under my wing. I also needed her badly. 'You can write a letter if you like and I will take it to the Hearing.' The first thing I did was close myself in a room and start writing from my heart. The following day I received a call from where the Panel was taking place. I was told she won't be back as Tynepark refuses to have her and she has nowhere to stay. I said 'she can stay with me'. 'In your house?' 'Yes' I said. 'We will need to discuss this' the reply was. 'It is possible but as she is not sixteen, Tynepark will call periodically in person to see how she is.' She arrived by train in the afternoon. We had an Alsatian dog that never ever went out onto the road but she went out on the road end, went a few yards down to meet her. I walked out. She had her riding gear on. I never mentioned anything about the whole incident, not ever. I just said, 'a ride is getting ready to go and you ride a particular horse called Solomon and help me on the ride.' I could write a whole chapter of her life with us. Which could in fact be my second book.

Anne did very well in Ireland, sat her Instructor's exam, passed and came home after being there one year with her B.H.S.I. This means she uses this behind her name to show she is a qualified riding instructor, a British Horse Society qualification. I now registered our school with the British Horse Society which meant we had an inspector from their headquarters in Basingstoke down south come unannounced each year to check the standard, watching two lessons, checking all the riding hats we supplied to the customers to wear when riding, all the tack checked for any stitching coming loose, checking the horses for shoes or saddle sores, feeding, grassland etc.

We came out in the 1st year as the top riding centre in Scotland. I was Proprietor and did all the office work, accounts, entry for exams as students from other centres came to sit their exams as we were now an exam centre.

Anne was Head Instructor. She had two students permanently working with us and training for their Instructor's Certificates. She trained many students with hundred percent pass rates. I had put up an indoor arena for her coming home and bought a top-class horse for her to compete.

We worked very well together, never ever fell out. My next idea was to run monthly shows for juniors and seniors. This was a great success. We now called our business Equestrian Centre rather than Riding School. I used a building attached to the house to open a cafeteria for the riders and spectators, another two buildings attached to each other used to be for the dairy. I opened a shop selling riding wear, jodhpurs, boots, knitwear, riding hats, etc. In the one next door to my office was one with telephone answering machine etc. All very successful, a lot of hard work.

In 1972 when Anne qualified, we carried on going from strength to strength. I also started a Riding Club with monthly meetings. We visited other centres. We had ladies ride outs, quiz nights, question nights with us on the panel in a hotel; we ran barn dances, dinner dances, etc. We did not have ride outs anymore after the indoor school - it was entirely teaching and when we did ride outs, we had a group of four boys in their teens who came from Edinburgh every Sunday morning. I used to notice Anne would be riding along next to one of them in particular. This was before she went to Ireland. When she came back it seemed this boy came down a few times to see her and so it transpired in 1978, he asked our permission to marry her. He was now a qualified Civil Engineer. A big decision had to be made. The wedding took place in November 1978. I offered them our home and we would find another but our new son-in-law was independent and decided to get planning permission to build his own house on a site which he got and more or less built the bungalow single-handed with one fellow helping.

I still kept control of the business for two years to see how Anne could cope without me being totally involved. She was more than capable. Her husband had his own work. We then decided to move from the Equestrian Centre and give it over to them.

Part Three

Disabled Riding

As Anne had experience of instructing disabled riders when she taught them at The Drum Riding for Disabled Centre for some time and felt fulfilled by this, and as she had a real heartfelt care for them, I thought we could try this for the East Lothian area or further afield, which again became very successful. We did have very quiet horses and ponies which were essential, plus we needed the helpers, 3 people to each animal, one to lead and one at the side to hold them on. Safety was important. We managed to get thirty helpers plus our staff. We had a hundred and eleven riders weekly and had a schedule of different times over the week for each group plus helpers.

I personally welcomed the parents who brought them along, some in wheelchairs, and Anne was in charge of the riders and helpers. The parents had seats in the gallery to watch the class. I would chat with the mothers to encourage them, as it is very difficult to have a disabled child.

I remember one particular day when I asked them how they felt when they discovered after the birth there was a problem. They all agreed on the same feeling. They were distraught to hear this. They questioned themselves, went back over the pregnancy to see if they could think of anything they had done that could have caused this. They felt ashamed and then the feeling came that they would fight tooth and nail for this child to get a chance in this difficult situation in the world. It really gave me a feeling of thankfulness to have had two normal daughters and huge sympathy and admiration for those mothers. We were the only place in East Lothian for disabled riders.

I was asked to come and give a talk about what we did, etc at various places who then all donated to us, as it was all free to riders, but obviously we had to buy extra saddles, etc. and extra ponies.

I spoke at the lunch time meeting of Tranent Rotary Club which was held in Tranmore Hotel, Tranent, and the outcome was they bought a new saddle and stirrups for us. The President and Vice-President came down to the indoor school and presented them to me. A picture was taken of this with Anne and her head girl standing with me.

I was also invited to talk at the Masonic Club in North Berwick and got a £200 donation. Also, I was invited to Ferranti's, a large factory outside Dalkeith. I got a cheque for £500 from them. All those presentations were photographed and put in the local papers. I also have photographs of them.

With the £500 cheque I received from Ferranti's, I bought a quiet pony from George Tait at Gifford from the field I now rent at the Glebe, Gifford. I never realised then that one day this would be ground I would rent. Life takes some strange turnings. I used our trailer from the school and brought the pony to his new surroundings. I called him Charity as I thought this was an apt name.

There was a chap from North Berwick called Frankie who was disabled but was keen to learn to ride, which we managed to do. He was taught privately with great determination and patience and care from us. He became very capable. He did get sore, but he felt he could cope with that. He was so appreciative. He wanted to give us something back. He said 'I would like to ride into North Berwick leading The Ride with some of your other riding customers behind me and raise money for your disabled section of your school". Also, he wanted to sell tickets for a dance at night after The Ride called 'Frankie's Sponsor Dance' to be held in Aberlady Hall.

The horse boxes, trailers, etc transported the horses down to the Queens Hotel car park in Gullane and the ride started from there, Frankie leading with the new pony called Charity. Our staff girls, two of them, had money tins collecting along the street, going on the bus at one end of North Berwick and getting off at the other, collecting on reaching North Berwick. The Ride stopped outside the Castle Hotel in Dirleton and the owner, Douglas Stewart, came out with drinks for the riders and a donation - also their customers donated. On reaching North Berwick, they rode down to the harbour where the Fire Brigade met them with a donation. Riding along Forth Street and High Street and up to the station car park where the horses were loaded up and taken back to the Centre. It was a very successful day and also sold out of tickets for the dance in the evening.

With the money raised, I went along to Lady Fayrer. owner of Overhailes Riding Centre and bought a block of disabled toilets from her which had ramps for wheelchairs and was so useful for mothers, taking their children to the toilet. I also got some new fencing and a gate for our field for the horses. We ran the disabled riding for two and half years.

Meantime the other side of the business was growing so much. Our school was a training exam centre. We had full time students, plus the whole centre was getting busier and busier. As well as training the students, the exams were being held on our premises, the students from other schools sometimes coming over from Ireland to sit the exams.

We felt we could not keep the Disabled Riding going, much as we did enjoy the time spent with the disabled riders One of our helpers was Jill Morrison from West Fenton, a farmer's wife. We approached her to see if she would take over at her farm. She agreed and is still going after all those years. "Muirfield Riding Centre" is very well known.

A lady in the church the other day said she had a message for me from Frankie Johnston. She obviously is a very good friend of his as he had been best man at their wedding. He is now in a nursing home in Bonnyrigg and she visits twice a week as she is a W.R.I. member at Athelstaneford. I had been asked last year to be one of their panel members. They had put questions together for each of us in turn to give our opinion. She had obviously been telling Frankie about this and he said 'I know that lady. Tell her I am asking for her". Both my daughter and I have sent cards to him with some news. I found one of his dance tickets and a photograph of him on Charity at Appin which I enclosed. I will make a point of visiting him now I know where he is. Life is amazing how it often goes the full circle. It is many years since I saw Frankie.

I feel so blessed to have had the good health to be able to reminisce and keep in contact with so many friends I have met along the way. I do hope I can keep driving for a bit longer as it gives me the independence to do what I like when I like.

In the local village of Drem, there was vacancy for Postmistress in the Post Office and General Store. I applied, was successful against many applicants. A house was attached and my next career started.

Part Four

Village Postmistress

When my daughter got married, I felt she had many years of teaching and training students behind her and decided I would let her manage the Riding School but I would still be owner which meant I would move near at hand, if possible, but give her the reins as it were.

It so happened at that time the post of Village Postmistress was vacant as the previous one was retiring. A house was attached which you would have to rent from the local farmer if he thought you would be a suitable tenant. Therefore, my first move was to see the farmer who was well known to my husband and my Father-in-law before and had had farming deals there. He said he would be happy to rent if I was successful with my application. The next step was to apply to the Head Postmaster at North Bridge, Edinburgh with my application. I knew there had been five applications in all, but I was picked so now the move was into the flat. A shop was attached to the Post Office and I had always wanted my own shop. I was delighted with my new challenge. I did have a lot to be responsible for as Pensions and Family Allowances and Post Office Savings Accounts meant you were holding a lot of money that was not yours and if you did not balance on balancing day, each Friday, you had to put in your own money.

The shop was very busy as it was all farm cottages in the village or railway workers. Wives did not drive. They depended on me for all groceries, milk, bread, papers, etc. The women from neighbouring farms and small holdings cycled or came pushing their prams. I used to go to the cash and carry 3 times a week, always in the evening, as I was open until 6.00pm. I started by bringing in the papers that were dropped off by newsagents from the doorstep at

5.30am. I took them in at 7.00am, got them sorted out for the regulars, opened the shop at 7.30 – 8.00am for people going to work and put some on the windowsill for the ones who were a bit later and their magazines. I closed from 8.00am till 9.00am, had my breakfast and did some housework.

I had a cigarette traveller every week, Dunbar lemonade lorry twice a week and a baker every day. I really was needed and if sometimes a People's Friend or My Weekly, etc was still on the windowsill, I would be away to that house to see if they were all right as no farm worker's wife had a telephone. I could get in touch with their families somehow. I often put on fires for them, made food sometimes, slept there all night if they were widowed and had no one near at hand. I have often packed a bag for hospital during the night and gone in the ambulance with them. I held keys for four or five people in the village so that I could get in if they were on holiday and their alarms went off.

I was the one the Police would phone and I would have to meet them with the key, day or night. If they were not very able to collect their Pension, I would take it to them. I would put milk and bread in for people coming back from holiday. I usually added a small vase of flowers as a welcome. I was also a Telegram Office and had to deliver the telegrams and see if there was a reply. If there was a wedding in the village I just had to close the door and go and deliver it. I remember there was quite a large farm house with a huge garden and the daughter was marrying a foreign chap. On that particular day, I was there eight times. They kept offering me a refreshment which I made sure was lemonade each time I accepted.

I was thoroughly enjoying my new work and my new house. I decided after two years of my daughter being manageress at the Riding School she was more than capable. She was expanding and doing very well competitively on her own horse, a Scottish Champion twice over, so I thought the time was right to pass the business on to her.

We had a huge garden at the Post Office premises which my husband had a great interest in. In fact, unknown to us, someone had taken a photograph and it was in the East Lothian Calendar one year with the garden and over twelve acres of glebe land on which we had sheep, cattle and sometimes crops.

We were both very busy but were enjoying our change of life. The early years of me taking over were such interesting times where I had lived so near before and knew a lot of people, and the village was so interesting, and I enjoyed chatting with all the different characters.

There were quite a lot of elderly people as the farmer never put any widow of his workers out of their houses if their husband had served him well. He was different from most farmers since they were in what were called tied houses. They would have to go but if they were widowed he would say 'You just stay where you are'.

There were two widows in the farm cottages who worked in the farmhouse. The farmer was on his own, a widower; one did the washing, cleaning, scrubbing etc, the other whose husband had been the gardener did all his personal work, like mending his underwear, making and changing his bed etc. He was rather shy having no children of his own. He would buy around six boxes of Black Magic chocolates at Christmas time from me and say 'It is handy when you visit at this time – just to lay a box on the table'. He then would tell me to make up two boxes of groceries, chocolates, etc and deliver them to the two ladies who worked in the house for him. He would not hand them over himself. I would deliver them and say who they were from. He was a very kind man. He renovated quite a large part of the house for us 'to make it comfortable' he said. I knew everyone so well in the cottages in Drem - all different characters. I enjoyed talking to them all. They always had stories to tell me.

There was a lady in her seventies who lived on her own, well educated, had been in the Wrens during the war and had been at Bletchley Park on the wireless (which gave the information of secret details of the war). Next door was a man in his seventies who lived on his own, both having lost their spouses. They used to talk to me about each other as if they despised each other but I knew differently as they were regularly chatting and visiting from time to time and when the lady would say to her neighbour 'I am going on the train today'. 'Oh, what time will you be back?' 'I will get the 10 o'clock to go to Edinburgh and come back on the 3 o'clock.' 'Ok. I will pop in and put your fire on about 2.45pm'. She always had it set with the sticks and coal. Davy, as he was called, would wait until he saw the 10 o'clock train go then in he would go, light Christine's, fire and pull in his chair. He spent all day burning her logs and coal and then pop back about 2.45pm to his own house – that did make me smile. Christine was furious one day when she came round to the Post Office telling me that Davy had got up with his pyjamas and dressing gown, brought his milk in from the doorstep, looked at

Christine's door and the milk was there so he picked up the bottles, went in and then came out again. Now Christine's door stood on the side of the road that led up to the farm steading. She imagined the men having to pass her door from their houses to the farm could have seen Davy coming out of her house in his pyjamas and dressing gown and think he had spent the whole night there and was going back in the morning to his own house. I did find that so funny. Davy came round a lot for his shopping with a lovely little basket. I always admired it. He told me it was a hundred years old. When he had to move to a care home, he came round and gave me the basket as he knew I liked it a lot. I still have it.

Another widower used to come for his Woodbine cigarettes every day also from the farm cottages. He was also in his seventies but knew he had his cottage as long as he was alive. He told me he had smoked Woodbine since he was nine years old and it had never done him any harm. He used to play his fiddle a lot. When the doctor called monthly to see the elderly, the doctor always played a tune on his fiddle as he was a fiddler also.

There was a mother and daughter in one of the council houses; the mother was in her nineties and had had her own house and tobacconist shop in Edinburgh and her daughter was the private secretary to the owner of the tannery where the sheepskins were treated in Haddington and they could go to be rugs, etc. Both of them were very refined ladies. The daughter had a wonderful sense of humour and loved telling jokes, much to her mother's disgust, but they were wonderful companions. The daughter had been engaged for thirty-six years to a farmer but they never married. She told me she would not have made a good farmer's wife and he was happy with a woman and mother who looked after him very well. My husband looked after their garden and I became very friendly with them. They had Post Office Savings Accounts and they had their rent to pay the Council each month; also Council Tax and their Pension to get. They trusted me so well they gave me their card for their bank account and I automatically withdrew their rent and Council Tax and paid it monthly whenever it was due. If they wanted money, they phoned me. I withdrew it and took it along to them, making sure I had every pay-in slip and withdrawal slip. They always said 'we do not need that'.

The daughter hated hospitals so, when her mum got unwell and had to go into hospital, I did the visiting and then she had to go into a care home when she was dying. I slept at their house so as I could go down during the night with the daughter. However, it was the next morning when we got word at 8.15am to come, but the daughter would not go. I had to open the shop at 9.00am but was only part-time by then, closing every day at 1.00pm. I had to go and empty all the drawers and bring everything home and take a principal part at the funeral.

I was always willing to help my customers in any way I could. They used to confide in me quite a lot about their personal life - which they knew I would never pass on. One lady in the village had a husband with dementia. She was asked the same question over and over again - up to twelve times. She said this particular day (and it was only midday) he had said 'does the baker's van come today?' and she was so exasperated she came to my door, dropped her shopping bag on the floor and just cried. I did my best to talk with her, and she then said 'I had better get back. I am afraid he puts the kettle on the electric cooker and it is an electric kettle or he had the hoover out and gets it in bits. I did so feel for her. I went round the corner, gave her a cuddle and saw her leave on her way. I also filled a lot of forms up for people, insurances for their homes or if they had a car or to do with family allowance, etc.

One gentleman who lived on his own in one of the farms would bring all his post to me and let me see it. He had a car that needed changed and I did all the paperwork about Road Tax, Insurance, etc. I always said after I had asked any personal questions 'you just sign, leave the form with me and go home and relax. I shall do the necessary and post if for you and you will get a reply in a few days'. It was a worrying thing for these people who had not been used to it. Life was at a slower pace in these days. They were down to earth, hard-working, humble people. The school children would get off the bus in the village from the High School, come in with their pennies and get a lollipop or a bar of toffee, etc. It all added up. The farm workers used to stop their tractors if they were passing, especially around their lunch break and come in and get a hot pie or sausage roll. It was a very good baker that delivered every day. I used to put a few in my oven about 11.45am knowing that workers would come in around 12 noon. The farmer grew a lot of carrots and when it was lifting and cleaning time for them, he would hire people, around fourteen of them. They would all come down at lunch time and get their pies, etc – good for business.

I had huge orders for the baker at Christmas and New Year time. On the eve of these dates I was so busy making up the orders of mince pies, Christmas cake, shortbread, etc I was always exhausted by the time I closed the door knowing I had two days off following this. I always had all the family on Christmas Day so after some tea and a sit down on Christmas Eve, it was last minute of parcelling presents for my family, Getting table prepared with glasses, crackers, etc., going to the Midnight Christmas Eve Service at the local Church, home for a cup of tea, giving my husband his card and present and him doing the same for me, off to bed, rise early and prepare the Christmas lunch!. Great times. It was a similar routine for New Year shop-wise and family-wise. We never went out for a Christmas meal to a restaurant in these days. The children got all excited with Santa's presents then got dressed up for their Grandparents, coming all excited to show them what they had got and knowing Granny and Grandad would have another present.

There was a time when the best Post Office in Scotland was to be picked by the customers picking up a form which was lying on the counter of every Post Office for them to fill in to say what they thought were the reasons for their Post Office to be the best. They had to fill it in and post it by a set date. I never gave it another thought when the closing date had been as I knew I was a small place in Scotland. I was absolutely amazed when one day I got a telephone call from the Headquarters to say I was in the final five. I

it was decided there were to be five finalists. The five were Pitlochry, Oban, Dundee, Granton-on-Spey and me, Drem - this was taken out of two thousand Post Offices. They gave me a date when they told me the result - which was Pitlochry the winner and I was the runner-up. No comparison, with all the customers and holiday-makers

Pitlochry had compared to me - mainly local regulars. I was told the officials would be down to take photographs of me and the Office and present me with a Certificate and take me out for lunch at the local hotel. They said the local newspaper would be here and also The Scotsman, taking photographs.

They also told me about one of my customers saying why she had recommended me that had overwhelmed them and put me in this position. So, they wanted that customer to be there too at my Presentation, taken at the Post Office door. I was told by them it was what I had done for this customer on a winter night when I was closed and it was so bad with snow. No cars could get out for the snowdrifts. The lady customer was also taken for lunch with us. I also got £200 as part of my prize.

The story from the customer was as follows. On this particular night she was in the house on her own with her small sons aged seven and nine. Her husband was away for a few days. She had a meter that took electric tokens to supply her electricity. I sold the tokens in the Post Office. At about 6.30pm I got this phone call from this lady who lived approximately one and half miles away to say she had no tokens and they had run out of electricity - no light, no fire, she could not boil a kettle, etc. and she was on her own. My husband was away down the road somewhere trying to help someone else dig their car out of a snowdrift. I asked her 'Is there any way you could walk along. I will open my safe, etc and give you the tokens although I am not supposed to do this after hours'. She said she would try and walk. She did arrive having left the two boys in the dark in the house. I told her to sit down for a minute. I still had bread and cake left from our tea on the table. I got her a hot cup of tea, unlocked all my Post Office doors, put off my alarm, opened the safe and gave her tokens. My husband had then just come in. I asked him if he still had his wellingtons on and waterproofs and if he would walk back with the lady and be sure she got back to her boys, which he did in strong wind and snowing all the time. I felt so grateful I was in a position to help but never imagined the publicity it gave me in The Evening News.

I had my picture taken headed **May 1st Class Post**. Every time the papers were going to print something about the closure of small post offices coming and what a miss it would be to the community, they would get in touch with the head office in Edinburgh and ask what small office would they recommend to have a picture taken to put in the paper with the article and they always said mine was to be the one.

I would get the call to have a customer outside leaving the Post Office with me saying 'Goodbye' to them. Sometimes it would be a case of asking another customer to come round and have a bicycle outside the window to show she had cycled to the Post Office. Another time a customer leaving with her stick showing she had walked being aided by her walking stick. The other offices in the vicinity and county could not understand why it was always me being chosen, being so small and against all the country offices in Scotland. The setting was good as we kept the garden and office immaculate but I had won the award as runner-up in Scotland against Pitlochry being the winner which was more of a town office. I presume I am 'a people person' and dedicated to my job.

The Head Post Office in Edinburgh would periodically send me letters from people who had been on holiday and who had popped into my office and who had had such a lovely welcome and in a beautiful setting and they should pay a visit to Drem and see for themselves.

On another occasion they telephoned me from Head Office and said I was getting a visit from Eileen McCallum who acted on Take The High Road at 11.00 o'clock one morning. She acted as Postmistress in a village and she wanted to visit a real village Post Office. Who would they recommend? Again, it was me. She thought it would help her to act in her role. That was to be recorded at 6 o'clock on the radio that evening on Scottish News, detailing our conversation. The reporter, who was a young lady, came from the BBC and recorded our conversation with me behind the counter and Eileen on the other side as the customer. She mimed and looked at us one by one as she wanted us to speak. My photograph was taken again and put in the paper. I have one in my living room. After the reporter left, Eileen and I had coffee together. The photograph is of both of us standing at the Post Office door.

I have received letters from people from abroad who had called and said how much they had enjoyed the welcome and chat they had had with me. I can honestly say that every day as Postmistress, no matter what was going on in my own life, everyone was greeted and departed with a smile. I cannot say I never had difficult customers but I never made any difference. I felt more sorry for them with that attitude rather than any form of anger.

We were allowed six weeks holiday per year. I never ever took that amount. I went for long weekends when it was a Monday holiday or perhaps used two weeks sometimes. I had to select the person who I wanted to take over. I usually selected someone who was running a husband and wife team with general store and Post Office. One was happy usually to come and have the extra money. I was totally responsible for that situation – if the books had not balanced, the Post Office rules were that I would have to replace the amount – no excuses were accepted. Luckily, I never was in that position. It was always an anxious time each balancing day which originally was a Friday. We were open until 5.30pm then we had to start counting - it meant a lot to me as my husband and I attended many dances on a Friday evening which usually started around 7.00pm. If we had not finished it all before we had to leave, I used to start again around 11.00pm and was often still in the office at midnight. Every pension and family allowance, all stamps and electric tokens had to be counted. I would not have been able to sleep if I did not know the answer. I have seen me recount pensions and family allowances two or three times over as often I had missed something. It was all done by hand – no computer or adding machine. The time did come later when the computer was installed in 2000. Up till then from 1978, it was all written out by hand.

It was hard work learning the computer. We had various training places to go – hotels in Edinburgh, the Marine Hotel in North Berwick. It was so much quicker when you got the hang of it and it meant that Head Office in Edinburgh knew exactly day by day what was happening. With this advancement, it meant we did not get as many unannounced auditors coming in. Some mornings, when I got up and was getting ready for work, usually 8.30am, I would look out of the window and a red car would be in the car park. Next minute, knock on the door. Audit today.

They dived at the cash first and then they went over everything else. The cash was always first before we opened at 9.00am, then they went to the back of the office and counted everything else. Luckily, I never ever had a bad audit. Some offices had embezzled Post Office money to start their shop or for their own use, sometimes totalling thousands which was beyond their control to pay back. So, they just had to hold up their hands in guilt and were sacked on the spot plus taken to court. I think at least two I knew and I was always with them at evening Post Office meetings - which were held in a hotel in Edinburgh - and they always maintained they knew all the answers and were always questioning the Chairman, etc. They were eventually glad to see the auditors and admit it as I think they were having sleepless nights and had no chance of replacing the money. However, computers did away with all that system as it was easy to keep giving false totals as long as no auditors appeared. They got used to knowing the ones to visit regularly. It was sometimes a year before I saw them.

Eventually the village changed a lot as the older people who had been left with their farm cottages died and the farmer retired. The cottages were sold to private owners who mostly had cars and wives who drove. This meant I did not have the same demand or need for the shop. Supermarkets had started and people were working in Edinburgh and they could even get stamps in newsagents or grocers on their way home. Then the steading of the farm plus grounds were taken over for housing - again all privately owned. By this time the small Post Offices were all put on the part-time opening from 9.00am till 1.00pm. After much consideration I decided I was compensating the shop. Menzies newspapers which were delivered every morning had to be paid by a Thursday and if not, you would not get any others. They kept putting in more and more magazines of all types which were on sale or return but you were charged for them all so they had to be paid for in advance. I could sell very few. I did run accounts for the papers for my customers and it was alright for the ones who paid weekly but I had a few farmers who had The Scotsman every day plus farming magazines and they wanted 3-monthly accounts.

It was a lot of pressure on me, so I decided to stop the shop and luckily a young chap and his wife came to live in the Station Master's house and were starting to try and sell sandwiches to the people going on the trains and were anxious for something else. So I asked him to take over the newspapers which he did – a great relief.

After having no shop for quite a few years when the new private houses were built in the farm steading – twenty of them - I thought maybe this could be an opportunity to start up the shop. I went over and visited them and asked them if they would be interested and it transpired only if I opened at 7.00am and sold milk and rolls which were two things which they had to have fresh daily. I could see a lot of wastage and most houses were empty all day as people were working and travelling to Edinburgh. I realised there was no longer a need apart from one lady who said 'you would be handy for the odd packet of biscuits'. I said I could not survive on that.

It now came to pass that all the sub-Post Offices would be made part-time, closing at 1.00pm each day. I was pleased about that as I was also interested in the farming side and my husband had sheep and cattle on the land we leased and

I could go and help in the afternoon especially at lambing time. In fact, when that was on we would get up and go to the field at 6.30am and check them all, often having to help some to lamb. We would easily spend two hours or more and I would say we must get down to Drem and let me open the Post Office. Of course, I had a different outfit for the farm job – wellington boots, working trousers and jacket – sometimes arriving back at 8.50am or even three minutes to 9.00 and I would jump out of our truck, kick off the wellingtons, off with the work clothes into the Post Office gear and open the office. I always dreaded the thought of a customer standing outside waiting on me. Luckily that never happened.

On reflection, I also became an Avon representative while still running the Post Office. I had the Avon brochures each month which I delivered to my customers who were in the Athelstaneford, Gullane and Drem areas. I left them for a week or so and gave them time to study and see if they wanted to place an order. I gave the date I would collect the brochure, also the date I would deliver the goods.

I did very well on this; my best customer was my daughter, Anne. She gave me a good order each month, not for herself only but for delivery to Bethany Christian Trust for the young women and girls who were being cared for in the houses and homes. The representative Director of Bethany from Pencaitland would call and meet here to collect soap, deodorant, perfume, tooth brushes, toothpaste, combs, etc. I was top seller for the Lothians and was presented at a hotel, The Grosvenor near Haymarket, at a Special Presentation for top sellers. I got a gold pen and a silver case with a good quality Manicure Set and a

Certificate. My daughter is a very kind and caring person and has helped so many people who have fallen on hard times. All I have written has been quite fulfilling to me over my thirty-two years.

There was one occasion that was the opposite. I had a break-in one evening. It was on 29th November, I remember as St Andrew's day was the next day and my husband was very patriotic. He always hoisted the St Andrew's Flag on our flag pole which was near the roadside in our car park on 29th and the first cars passing to work on the morning of 30th would see the flag. On this occasion, he was working, being hired with his own tractor to go to the Mushroom Unit at Fenton Barns each day from 4.30pm after the pickers had finished, until 8.30pm. I would prepare the evening meal for him coming home.

I was cooking the meal and discovered that I had no salt. My parents had retired and bought a house just on the back road behind me. I decided to take my car out of the garage and go round to get some salt. I had reversed the car back a bit and thought I had a soft tyre. We had an electric pump. I was blowing the tyre up and thought I heard my phone ringing in the house and then thought 'no I think it is the noise of the pump'. I spent around twenty minutes with them and motored back round. As I was entering my opening to come into the car park, I noticed my house was in darkness. I looked at the houses opposite me and their lights were on. I had a terrible feeling as some other Post Offices had been targeted by break-ins. I really panicked as I had sold an older type of car for £900 and had the money in the Post Office safe. I had the keys on me – I never left them in the house if I was not in. One was for the house door to get in, one for going from my living room to the Post Office and the other one for the safe. I was always so careful. I slept with them under my pillow. The Post Office emphasised to always be careful and keep your keys safe.

In my panic I ran to the Post Office window and could hear the shuffling and noise. I knew they were in there. I then ran to my house door and tried it. It was locked by a huge lock and key from the inside which I never used as I had a Yale lock that I used and therefore it was no use as they had evidently turned on the larger one.

I then went back to my parents and phoned for the police. Then I came back round and asked a neighbour to come over with me. We discovered they had entered by the back bedroom window. The police arrived and said as they passed an opening on their way towards the Post Office a blue van had come out of the opening - they reckoned that must have been them. They had evidently parked the van and then crossed the field and got into my house at the back. I think it had been my telephone ringing to see if I was in as the telephone kiosk is just behind here and me not answering and the car away was the problem.

I had an alarm system on the Post Office with the main part above the front door of the office. They had dismantled that without it going off and we found it in the garden later. The police said one of them must have known how alarms work. They had burst the lock from the sitting room through to the Post Office. The previous owner had a drawer full of keys in the office. They had them all scattered on the floor having obviously tried each one to get into the safe which is built into the wall. It was a fire place at one time and was cemented all round it with a heavy iron door. This was done by the previous owner. They had gone into our shed and got a heavy metal bar and had been trying to remove the concrete around the safe. The whole floor was covered in papers emptied out the cupboard. My bed was turned upside down, handbags all emptied, washing machine emptied, all cabinets in the living room emptied. Luckily their being disturbed and not getting the safe open was a relief as I imagined my own money gone.

The place was in a turmoil, the police were still there when my husband came home, seeing the police cars. I felt completely exhausted and thought I would need to get up early tomorrow morning and tidy up all the papers and mess that were lying on the Post Office floor before the customers come in for their papers.

I was up at 6.00am and also Duncan who disappeared outside so I thought this is fine, he will be getting a sack to put all the papers, etc that are across at the customers' counter side. He came walking in with nothing. I said, 'I thought you would be bringing in a bag to lift this lot'. 'No' he said, 'I was putting the flag up as I did not get it done last night'. I said 'that is right, we have had a break-in. Put the flag up'. I did say he was patriotic, but that was taking it beyond. We did have a laugh about that bit. They did not get anything but I said to the police I was worried in case they come back. He said that, no, they did not get anything tonight but they may get £20,000 tomorrow night elsewhere.

I got a letter from Head Office saying how sorry they were to hear of the break in but congratulating me on being so careful with the keys. I still am even though I no longer have the Post Office. Wherever I am the keys are with me.

The police told me later on they did get them in a caravan at Berwick doing another two offices, but they could only charge them with the ones they caught them at.

I felt very vulnerable when I was left on my own and was still running the Post Office as it does stand back by itself but now that I no longer have the Post Office I know the temptation is not the same. I do enjoy the privacy of my house and garden.

My husband started to feel not very well with a lot of shoulder and back pain. He went to the doctor and was told it was pleurisy, but it got worse and he had to go to the Western Infirmary for a scan. Bad news. It was his lung and was Mesothelioma cancer from working with asbestos – it was very painful and there was no cure. It will never show up under twenty years and can take up to forty years. He had cut some asbestos when building a shed early on in our marriage. What a blow and anxiety for both of us and our two girls. The prognosis was that he would not last very long. He did not want to be in hospital and said he wanted to be at home with no visitors and for me to look after him, to which my reply was 'if that is what you want that is certainly what we will do'. It was a very difficult time as I was working in the Post Office as well. One daughter previously had all the trips of taking him to hospital for tests, etc. and the other one did all the shopping and getting prescriptions. I just stayed and attended to him, popping through from the Post Office regularly. I was giving him the morphine with a syringe as he had to have it as a break from pain during the night on the top of his daily doses. I was up sometimes eight, ten or even twelve times one night and still could not kill the pain.

It turned out that the tumour started to grow outwards, instead of inwards which meant they could not say how long he would have. They could not understand it. I felt I did my bit as I prayed very night to give me time as he was adamant he wanted a burial and was to be buried in his wedding suit, which he always said was still there. All the sheep and cattle had to be looked after. Luckily my brother stayed near the field and kept an eye on it and phoned me regularly saying all was well. I am sure it was not always the case. The outcome was that he lasted almost three months. I was only out three and a half hours in that three months. He wanted me there. It was 6th December 1999 and I was getting sympathy cards, amounting to two hundred and thirty-six wreaths and Christmas cards all coming in at the same time. Plus, the Post Office had its busiest time of the year. However, you get the strength to do it and we were thankful he was at rest for his sake. He is a huge miss to me as we had a wonderful compatible marriage and the girls adored him – it was just us 4.

A new life completely for me. I still had to be behind that counter every morning and I think that was an asset rather than a bother or otherwise. I could have pulled the duvet over my head and just lain where I was. I realised how I was on a different par over these months. When I looked out the windows and saw the traffic passing I thought the world has been going on. I had never ever looked out the window or had even looked in the mirror. I felt strange and awkward when I went to North Berwick afterwards to shop and after ten minutes I had to get into the car and come home. I felt frightened to cross the street. The next week I asked my daughter to come to Haddington with me because I felt anxious, certainly no way was I ever an anxious person.

I then realised I must get myself occupied to keep my mind busy and not think so much. I went to help at St Mary's Church in Haddington as a Welcomer and also worked in the shop on Sundays. I also went as a Volunteer to Roodlands Hospital in the Cafeteria RNS Voluntary Service. I had my badge. I could do these things in the afternoon.

I had a very good friend - and still have locally - who lost her husband, also in farming, and my husband and him were very good friends and are buried in Athelstaneford New Cemetery next to each other. She lost her husband a few years earlier and we became very close when I was widowed. She was a tremendous help asking me to go for a weekend away together and this developed into us doing this many times in the years following, the Borders and Pitlochry being very popular.

I have two cousins, sisters, Louise and Marjorie, who stay in Edinburgh. They were my flower girls when I got married. I hardly ever saw them during my working life. We arranged we would meet in Jenners, Princes Street, in Edinburgh once a month, have coffee then one and half hours later have soup, and a nice cake and tea in another half an hour's time. We usually departed around 3.00pm after spending four hours non-stop talking.

After Duncan died, Louise and her husband had taken early retirement and bought a house in France. They invited me to come over and spend some time with them.

They were coming over to Ireland for their son's wedding and they wanted me to go back with them as they were spending a few days in Edinburgh. I arranged a relief for the Post Office. I had to cut it down to one week instead of two as I could not get a relief to do any longer. This was coming up for eighteen months after Duncan's death. My Dad lived in a house just behind the Post Office, Mum had already died seven years previously, so I was his carer - although he was healthy and fit, I was always there for him. He died in my kitchen a year before Duncan with a massive heart attack. One part of me was saying 'go to France' another part was saying 'can you really cope with this?'

My two girls convinced me to go – 'it will do you good'. By this time my brother was diagnosed with cancer. When I reflected on it all, keeping the Post Office going daily when all this was going on, I thought maybe I do need a change. I decided. The decision was right. I had the relief in place and I was booked. Getting nearer the date for leaving, preparations in office, outside, clothes, haircut and coloured, I am starting to look back and think of all I have worked through with Gifford, land and animals; John's illness; Post Office and the upset with robbery, etc. The day arrived. I was sitting up in bed writing down my thoughts at 3.30am. Sleep would not come. The girls were so supportive as always. I am so lucky to have them. Duncan's words were so true – thank goodness you have the girls.

The trip out to France was marvellous. As we approached, I thought the French Riviera is all it is praised up to be. I sat out in the garden and we had mostly all our meals out there - what a wonderful life Louise and Douglas had out there. It gave me a new vision and made me realise there is a whole large world out there. I had always been interested in French language at school and could remember quite a lot of the basics but trying to understand the very smart French ladies! They seemed to talk so quickly, I found it difficult. Louise had an evening party out in the garden on the Saturday when I met the neighbours. There were two girls aged fourteen there and they were having English taught to them, so I asked them to come up to the lemon tree in the garden which had a bench under it and I asked them a few things in French and they understood. They tried talking to me in English so we coped with each other. I came back after doing a lot of sightseeing and great hospitality – it was well worth the trip.

Life keeps moving on. I was so blessed by having my two wonderful daughters. They are so loyal and attentive. One being only five minutes' away and who pops in almost every day and the other one living near the ski slope in Edinburgh who phones most days and visits more or less every week. Duncan kept saying 'Thank goodness you have the girls'.

The Church connection was a great help. I went to the Guild regularly, also sometimes as Overseas Representative and attended the General Assembly and reported back to our Guild. At other times I was Secretary and a few times President.

My main objective was to keep occupied as much as possible. I often say to people who have experienced loss that there might be another way but that is the way I managed. It takes a long time to recover. I realised this when I looked out of my living room window and said to myself 'My goodness, that is Kilduff up there'. I said 'My goodness, I have never looked further than the bottom of my garden'. I was thankful for the mother and daughter in the village, whom I mentioned earlier having helped them a lot, as it was a house I could just walk into at any time. It was winter nights at the beginning of my being on my own when I would look round the walls and think I would go crazy if I sat here any longer. I would get up, put on my jacket and scarf and sometimes a hat as it was a cold evening and walk along. The old lady would be sitting in her chair and gave me such a welcome when she saw me and her daughter, also called Mae but a different spelling from me, would go and put the kettle on and we would chat.

They were a wonderfully close mum and daughter so the atmosphere was good. I would stay for up to two hours. Mae's sense of humour was wonderful – a bit crude sometimes – but funny. Her mum was very lady-like and would say 'Oh Mae'. I would come home thinking of the conversation and feel I could relax - a true saying what you put around you gets around.

We had planned to retire the year following Duncan's death but of course I did not want to retire after that. I still kept the sheep and cattle and spent as much time as I could there, still getting a bit of help from my brother. The girls wanted me to give them up and I said 'No, I will know when the time is right'. I remember when the lambing time was on, my brother telephoned me and said he and his wife would take me out to Juniper Lea Hotel near Soutra for a meal 'but don't go into the field on your way up to look at the sheep. I have looked at them and there is nothing going to lamb tonight'. We had a shed we brought them into when they were getting near lambing. So I went up and went out with them and left around 11 o'clock. I decided I would go and look at the sheep in the shed on the way home, not saying so to John. We had a few sections made with straw bales to give them a little bit of privacy. I had a skirt and my boots on -not wellingtons, dress boots – and a torch in the car. I climbed the gate, made my way downhill to the shed and had a look. Three ewes were in there and thinking as John said it would likely be over the week-end and this was Saturday, not tonight.

I noticed immediately one was in pain and would definitely lamb so I sat on a bale and waited and eventually she did lamb. When I had attended to her I looked at the one opposite and she had started so I waited again. She was eventually not managing to produce the lamb so I thought I needed to help here so I had to get down on my knees, get my jacket off, roll up my sleeves, get my hand inside her and feel the lamb. They come feet first and the one foot was bent over and this was holding up the process so I managed to turn it and all was well. I thought 'my goodness, the time must be getting on'. I had no watch on. I got myself back up to the gate - it was locked so I climbed over it again and into the car. I thought time must be getting on and then I said to myself, 'what does it matter. No-one is waiting for me even if I was out all night. No one would know'. When I got the door open, put on the light and looked at myself, my skirt was in some mess all mucky and wrinkled, the boots were muddy all the way up and it was 2.30am.

I had sat with these sheep for three hours in the dark with a torch going off and on now and again. I never told my brother about it. He telephoned me on the Sunday to say two sheep had lambed as if it had just happened. I did not want to say I know, I was there.

The better weather came on and the lighter evenings and I used to go up in the evenings. This particular evening some of the cattle had come through the fence into a part of the field they should not have been in. We were keeping it for hay so I chased them back and I fell into some nettles and again I was all dirty and stingy. I called in at my daughters and told her, 'I said I will know when the time was right to part with the stock. Well, as far as the cattle are concerned, it is now'. I washed my hands etc., went straight to my friend whose son was coming on to their farm and he had his own lorry and used to take his cattle to the market. So

I said 'Could you possibly take mine?' and he said he would. I still wanted to keep the sheep, much to my daughter's disgust, but I knew if I parted with them when I was ready I would never regret it. So I carried on with the sheep for the best part of another year but put them away before lambing.

I then let my daughter and son-in-law have the field to grow hay and silage for their horses' feeding each year, which they still do. I have never ever regretted doing that. I then found I had time and I found it easier to settle at home, do the Post Office in the mornings and my garden in the afternoon which is a huge garden with different sections of grass. I did get someone to cut my grass and hedges - it is more like an estate than a household garden - but I have a nice summer house and summertime is very pleasant.

I was beginning to hear there was talk and see in the newspapers that the village Post Offices were getting discussed about closing some of them. I was hoping mine would be one of them as I felt I was ready after serving thirty-two years and was now seventy-seven years old. Sure enough, it was not long before I heard from Head Office that an official would be coming to see me. Dirleton and Gullane Post Mistresses were also very keen for them to be closed but we knew it would not be all of us.

It was not long before I had a visit to discuss the position which was that they had been trying to find somewhere in or around Drem that could have the Post Office on their premises for one morning a week from 9.00am till 11.00am. They said 'we have not been successful so far and if we can't find anywhere to be a service to the community you will need to stay open. We do have one more place to try and it is the Appin Equestrian Centre'. I said 'my daughter and son-in-law own that'. 'I saw you had a lot of pictures in your living room of horses but did not know that. We will come back next week and have a chat with you after you have asked them' I thought that there was no way my son-in-law would agree to this. I mentioned it to my daughter and she asked him. Next day I asked 'did Raymond say no way?'. 'Why did you think that? He really did not say one way or the other'.

My other alternative was put to me by the Post Office. What if I would allow someone else from some of the bigger offices come and use my premises one morning a week? I did not like the idea of my being through the door of my living room hearing someone else on the premises. I lay in bed and thought it out at nights thinking the only thing I could do if I really wanted to close, which I did, was to go for my shopping over that two hours and not be around.

I was down to one day to go for decision time on the day they were coming when I got a telephone call from my son-in-law who worked for the Council in Haddington. He was at his work and he asked 'what time is your meeting at your office today?' I said '12 o'clock' and he said he would come down. I thought he was going to be in to hear if it gets heavy-going for me so I said with mixed feelings okay. He replied that if this meant the difference between me getting retired or not he would offer a building for them at the Centre. He had just built three new nice-sized brick buildings, one for staff having their lunch, etc, one for storage of horse feed and one he had not decided upon. The meeting went very well. Two men arrived this time. My son-in-law took them up, showed them around. They thought it was ideal. It was January and the arrangement was I could finish at the end of March. I was delighted.

It was quite a large job for my son-in-law. He had to lead the electricity over into the building put sockets in for computers, etc. and a heater. He is capable of doing all this himself. He put on a separate gate to enter and a notice was to go out on the roadside saying Post Office. The agreement was it would be a trial of five years - if there were not enough people using it, he would get his building back and that would cover that the facility had been there for the community. Gullane and Dirleton were disappointed as they had to carry on but now no Post Office and the same at both places.

I was now excited and started to plan that whenever I closed, I would go the very next week to the Orkney

Islands and stay as long as I wanted to see all the different mainland and islands where my ancestors had been farming mainly or fishing. I had managed to go twice, once with my husband and once with my brother and his wife, as John had also been born in Orkney. He had never been back and now he was sixty-five and retired. He had wanted to go but his wife would not fly or go by sea.

One day, when I had a few of our cousins visiting me and was doing a family tree and wanted some information, my parents now having been dead and I was the next in line, John asked to me 'if I went to Orkney would you come with me?' I said of course I would. 'Would Duncan come?' and I said yes. His wife, hearing this and knowing there was no stopping John this time, decided to come. We booked a lovely house for a week in Finstown and flew up. The house had the roof in the shape of a boat upside down and it was called The Boat House. We visited where we had been born, one on the mainland and the other on the Island of Rousay, found out it was still the same family that farmed there on both places and were still there with grandsons carrying on the business. We met quite a few cousins etc., with me being the one that approached the door, did the introductions and then waved the other three to come out of the car. It was a lovely week. My brother said 'I will never be back unless I come to stay as it would only be second best'.

When I was working, I could not get away very much and that visit was in 1998. I just longed to go back someday and have a longer time to really explore where my ancestors had been. I had a family tree that went back eight generations. All were Orcadians on both Mum and Dad's sides. I kept this wonderful plan that when retirement came, I would go off there to myself, as if you plan it and don't do it then it, can be that you never get there as you don't know what is around the corner and you may never do it.

I had kept in touch since the last time I was there with different cousins that I had visited and they were looking forward to me coming back and they offered me accommodation. I thanked them very much but also let them know that this was going to be more of an adventure than a holiday as I knew I would be going on different trips to different islands and the mainland. I wanted no restrictions this time.

My decision was that I would motor up with my own little Fiesta car to Thurso then cross on the Catamaran to St Margaret's Hope and drive from there for a start. My plan was that I would take no one with me as I felt if they are not Orcadian, they would not be interested or I would be asking them each day what would they like to do. NO. I was going to book nothing ahead at all, take my time, stop where I wanted, stay as long as I wanted and feel free as a bird after thirty-two years behind a counter. It seemed to be so wonderful. It kept me going for the months leading up to the closure.

I was presented with my special Certificate and a framed award with the Post Office logo at the top. Underneath the logo it stated:

We thank you for your service

MAY V.R.FAIRBAIRN

Congratulations!

ROYAL MAIL HONOURS YOUR 30 YEARS PLUS OF

SERVICE

WE THANK YOU FOR YOUR DEDICATION TO OUR

CUSTOMERS AND OUR BUSINESS

SIGNED

DONALD BRYDON	ADAM CROZIER
CHAIRMAN	CHIEF EXECUTIVE
ROYAL MAIL GROUP	ROYAL MAIL GROUP
(POST OFFICE)	(ROYAL MAIL)
PARCEL FORCE	

So ended my Post Office Career.

No regrets, glad I had the opportunity.

Part Five

Diary of my Holiday, Adventure on my Retiral

2009

26th April: I left Drem at 8.10am. Stopped for petrol at Stirling Services and phoned Fiona while there. She seemed so anxious about me taking this step. Then on towards Callander. I stopped three miles before Callander in a lay-by, had my flask of tea and three digestive biscuits. Moved on to Strathyre Forest and had a sleep in the car for one hour (I did not sleep well the night before at home). It was raining heavily all the way. Went into Strathyre Inn for a bowl of soup, far too thick - did not enjoy it. The Inn was established in 1720. It looked it too, really needed refurbished. Strathyre Station used to be opposite. Moved on to Glencoe and saw Duncan's cousin Paul and his wife - spent a nice afternoon with them - still raining heavily. I found a lovely hotel in Loch Leven looking out to the bridge called Loch Leven Hotel. I booked in for the night - felt I had driven long enough in the rain. The hotel was so comfortable. Food at dinner was excellent. I decided at dinner to book in for the following night also as the forecast was still rain.

On the morning of 27th, I phoned old dear at Appin and arranged to call on her around 1.00pm. On arriving at Appin, I thought I would visit the craft shop. I got talking to the owner and he informed me of his daughter events, Briony Lewis is her name. They stay over in Lismore but keep her horse at the Appin Centre. We were still deep in conversation when the door opened and he said to me 'this is the owner of the Centre' and we got introduced. He informed me that his mother ran the Appin Welsh Stud in 1978 and from there her son now has it. He has seven ponies, a few horses and treks mainly. His mother's name was McAlpine Downie. When he was told I had started Appin in East Lothian he said 'I know Anne has that. Anne Montgomery - I get her mail sometimes if it does not have a post code. The last one was a letter from America'. I said 'I hope it wasn't' a cheque'. He said, 'Sign for Centre' written Gaelic "*Letterskeou*". No, more like junk mail. 'I did have customers arrive one day saying they had booked previous to coming on holiday and were recommended to come to Appin.' After some argument we came to the conclusion it was 'Appin' in East Lothian. I said to myself 'I bet they are tearing their hair out waiting on this customer.'

I then proceeded to the old lady, Dolly - had a lovely time with her. She reminds me so much of Granny Fairbairn, cousins are amazingly alike, I have discovered on my travels. We spoke and laughed. She is not very good on her legs and has a home-help but she did want me to have a cup of tea, so I said I would make it. 'Right', she said and came through to the kitchen with her sticks and said she would direct the traffic, meaning she would tell me where to turn and which cupboard to open. If you can adapt to the old and the young, you can have so much fun and learn knowledge as well.

On my way back, I went into Duror Post Office, as I knew the husband of the lady who owns the Loch Leven Hotel has run this post office and store for two years. He is the exact opposite of her – very scruffy and untidy. I think she must have got him down there to keep him away from the guests. He told me he was going to give it up, definitely the Post Office side as he said he had never balanced since he started up. It was not the stamps that were wrong but the money, too much hassle. I am not surprised. He stands with a skip hat, looks untidy, has a load of rubbish at his feet behind the counter, loads of it for the customers to see. I asked 'how do you get on with the leaflets you have to introduce customers to insurance, etc?' 'Oh, I don't put any of them out on display. I just throw them at my feet with the rest of the rubbish. If someone opened an account with me I would not know what to do'. A bit of a dead loss certainly. Wouldn't encourage trade. I think the Post Office will be glad he is giving up. In my bed now at 9.00pm – still raining.

Tuesday 28th: left Hotel around 10.30am. Enjoyed good company last night. Was in Fort William within ½ hour of leaving hotel. I looked round the shops then made my way up to Invergarry and stopped outside a tea room on the road side. Laid back my seat in the car and slept for an hour then studied the map to see how far I would go and decided to go into the tea room, had some soup, tea and current cake. I moved on to Drumnadrochet, then Dingwall then on to A9 for Thurso. I had a bit of difficulty finding a bed and breakfast but one person phoned her friend and I got a little individual building (Previously outhouse for animals) with my own door into a beautiful garden - huge woodland part for a walk. Lovely evening. She had family staying in the house but I was the only booked B&B and she brought me a casserole on the house.

I went into the house for breakfast the next morning, nice breakfast. When I was finishing, the husband came through and he and I had a half hour chat. I told him my life experiences, he told me his. He had a few knockbacks while bringing up four daughters as at the same time, he was penniless but okay now. Very interesting. He gave a jar of homemade marmalade on leaving. His wife said 'we like to feel you arrive as a guest and leave as a friend'. I really enjoyed coming up Loch Ness with the broom out, sun shining and my Scottish tapes playing (this is the life)

A9 very busy. I was glad to get off it for a bit. I took the Wick fork rather than the Thurso one as I was going to visit Alex Clark's mother-in-law, who is Orcadian. I had a lovely afternoon with her, loads of stuff to eat as usual. I left her just after 6.00pm and decided I would make for John O' Groats Gills Bay and go over the next morning on the catamaran to Orkney. Again, had to find B&B as some had not started yet. My driving was well tested in Wick, up the High Street, over bridges, roundabouts, etc. I managed to find the street and house I wanted.

On entering, John O' Groats' facilities looked bleak. Some B&Bs I would not take, others full, two lots were old men running them. I ended up with one option, Sea View Hotel, about three miles from the boat. Not ideal. Everything mediocre apart from the price. They know how to charge up there. It was noisy, like central heating booming away all night. I looked under the bed twice during the night as another noise was going on. I did not know if it was mice or rats but did not find anything. I was checking electric plugs. The TV was six inches from the ceiling with a bar under it for coat hangers. You would have needed to be nine foot tall to reach them. No room for wardrobe. Good job I was excited about crossing to Orkney in the morning. I had a poor breakfast, as was the prawn cocktail the night before.

My sail was booked for 1.45pm.

A lovely day, sunshine but the wind is always cold as you are surrounded by the sea. I changed into my thick trousers, warm coat and hat, put on my sea bands and ready for the off. No problem on the crossing, sea fairly rough but sea bands great. Arrived at St Margaret's Hope at

2.45pm then drove to Lynfield Hotel as I entered Kirkwall - 4 star. Had a full suite, excellent food, real luxury. It cost me £75 B&B but the feeling of my first night in Orkney having planned it for so long, it was worth every penny.

I telephoned a second cousin I had not met but he knew I was coming up and he came to the hotel next morning and I followed him to his home. He had been the Captain on the Kirkwall to Aberdeen boat until he retired. He has 4 sons all at sea. One now is the captain of his father's previous boat, another one went to the Philippines and brought the catamaran home that I sailed on. His grandson I also met, is doing his Second Mate's ticket on the catamaran at the moment. I had a lovely time with Davy Pottinger and his wife Greta – coffee and soup and sandwiches later.

Then I moved on the Stomness Hotel and booked in for three nights as I had cousins and friends around there. Driving in Stromness is difficult as it has narrow streets, cobbled and flag stones and all so steep. I left the car in the car park at the back of the hotel on a slope and walked everywhere around Stromness doing my visiting.

Great hospitality, good conversation, many laughs, also felt I gained a lot of knowledge.

After I settled in on my first day at Stromness Hotel, which overlooks the harbour, I saw the New Hamnovoe boat coming in from Scrabster and Thurso to Stromness, which I had debated about taking over but felt as I was visiting Wick, the catamaran was quicker and nearer. I got my camera, hurried down the hotel steps onto the pier to photograph the boat arriving. As it straightened up for the harbour, it gave two hoots. I was totally overcome. I could hardly see through the lens of the camera for tears. I was thinking of my ancestors arriving home with such joy and leaving with sadness. I know they used to be met at the boat by the family and leave them again at the pier.

The Orcadians do not shake hands, kiss or cuddle when they meet. They wait outside their homes to meet you if they know you are coming. They would never wait until you rang the doorbell. They would say hello, smile and say 'come away ben'. Hospitality is wonderful and when you leave, they stand back outside and see you off with a 'cheerio' but no touching, that is the real Orcadian. I am sure the incomers will be different. My visits were all to the born and bred Orcadians.

I was finding my feet now and felt I had been to war and now I had come home. This is what I had dreamed about, wished and planned for and certainly was not disappointed. There must be some deep-rooted part within me. It certainly makes me feel <u>this</u> is where I belong. I went to Church when I was in Stromness. I felt it was for me. The theme of the service was Welcome Home – how appropriate was that, saying there may be many people now thinking of coming home as I did but could not tell you the circumstances in this building. I can imagine someone coming up through the Highlands, wondering what they are going to see when they eventually reach Orkney. Some may be disappointed, some surprised but others will have a real inner feeling of belonging, finding their own identity. The Lord knows our feelings and tells us to come home. We wander but he is always at home. I felt I had been chosen to go to this church that morning, just confirming what I felt and what I was doing in these lovely Orkney Islands. I was in their back part for coffee and I told the lady Minister that I felt this sermon was just for me. She put up both her thumbs. I felt she had been inspired to deliver that service for my benefit and probably for others as well. I met a girl from Newcastle when we were having our coffee at Church who was working for the RSPB, going around the Orkney Islands until August.

Later on, when I was having my Sunday Carvery in the Stromness Hotel, she came in for lunch, so I asked her to join me. We had a good chat. I could have spent longer with her but I had promised to be at another second cousin's (Johnnie Burgess's) house for 3.00pm and I was walking. They told me it would take around fifteen minutes. It was all uphill. It took me three quarters of an hour but what a great afternoon I had. He told me his life story – so interesting. For years he was only a name but to spend time was so interesting. Mum used to drag him to school as he hated it but he always ran home. She had to tether a calf at the roadside when she went to school and take it home with her when she came home. I walked back another way – it took me 1 hour – very breezy and cold. I was surrounded by water. But the memories of my lovely afternoon with a ninety-four-year-old man who does his own shopping and garden and walks most days really made me understand you are only as old as you feel. Back to the hotel, paid my bill as I am leaving in the morning. I think I will go to Hoy where my Dad and his ancestors belonged as far back as three hundred years.

Crossed over on Hoy Head boat around noon. Stayed in a lovely B&B, English couple. Blowing a gale - she could hardly hold the door open long enough for me to enter. Such a stylish place.

Next morning, went down to the area where Pa Pa and his Dad farmed, got two stones from his house, only a ruin now with two bundles of stones, stood on the ground where he worked and wandered around their ground. Also saw the hut, still standing, where Mum and Dad stayed when they first married. I went in some broken windows, otherwise two rooms, bathroom still there and kitchen. That was in 1931. The hut had been occupied by the military in the First World War 1914-1918. I met a lady who lived close by and was invited in. The second invite to stay by people I never knew before. She showed me a photograph of the house and also a school photo of North Walls school. The children were all numbered. It was taken in 1922 and Dad was in it. She promised to send me a photocopy of both. Dad would have been ten and he looked so like how I remember my brother Raymond at that age.

My B&B now on my second night in Hoy was the extreme opposite from the first. I had to travel to the very top of the island, driving several miles over moorland, a bit I had never seen before but also had heard my ancestors speak about - Rackwick area. It was a working farm, six cats, two dogs, quite rough. Had a good conversation, very different from the previous night but all in the tapestry of life.

The mother was at the foot of the road in the Post Office for twenty-nine years. She had been in the farm previously until she lost her husband. She opens when she is ready in the morning, sometimes after 10.00am. Her daughter-in-law, my landlady, sorts the mail when it comes off the boat, then delivers it. I got breakfast of a kind in between quite a funny set up doing so many things and nothing properly anyway. Paid my bill again and went down to see the Postmistress in her house. Had coffee and a yarn and went down for the boat again to take me back to the mainland. Did not want to go into a town again and stayed on a hill farm. The weather was arctic. I could not hold the car door open long enough to get in. I had to do it in stages. The accommodation was very comfortable.

I stayed two nights as I had a lovely sitting room and the lady said do not bother going out in this weather, stay in as long as you want - coffee in the sitting room and a meal each night. A very well-run farm, all cattle, machinery in first class condition. They had three sons, none was interested in the farm. It was a grandson that ran it with his grandad who was semi-retired. Phoned Kathleen, Mum's cousin, who has a farm at Skaeld Deerness, still on the Mainland. Going there tomorrow but going for a nice leisurely bath now and bed.

Driving wind and rain battering in the window. I am seeing a lovely highland mother and calf braving the storm outside the dining room window. Took a while to sleep last night as the wind was howling, although it was nice and warm in bed with an electric blanket and I had a whisky and lemonade before I went off. I never believed my soup was special but I have learned to believe it must be for I had many plates of soup at many houses and hotels and I always felt this should have been made different, a potato added or not boiled long enough. Often, you could stand your spoon up in it. Went to see Kathleen at Deerness and her family - had a nice afternoon. Another night on Hill Farm but I'm leaving in the morning. Going back to the Stromness Hotel as I am going out with a couple to see a farm mum used to work at.

Left farm this morning – wind still blowing hard and rain lashing. Got warm raincoat, thick trousers and warm hat on. Here goes! Had to lean forward to walk to the car - almost impossible – you could not hold the door open. You had to get one leg in and lean against the door and pick your time to quickly lift the other in. Quite an experience. You held the door by your knee and got it in between gusts. This is day ten since I arrived and I have worn the outfit I described every day. I have only worn two outfits since leaving home, so much for the two cases of clothes I brought. I came in to Stromness at 11.15am with my photos to be developed. If you are in by 11.15am you get them the same day at 5.20pm when they come off the bus from Kirkwall. Enquired about getting my hair coloured and blow dried at 9.00am at the hairdresser next to the Stromness Hotel where I am staying and they took me straight away - £32 and made a good job. I wanted it done before I go to stay at Scapa tomorrow for three nights with Brenda and Morris, Granny's cousin with another one, Mary, next door. Should be good farms.

Arrived at Brenda's and Mary's at 2.00pm, Saturday. Both waiting for me outside their porch – real Orcadians, great welcome but no touching. Nice smiles, hellos and come on ben. We had chicken and vegetables, potatoes and gateau. We were too busy chatting, the vegetables got burned. We did not mind.

On Sunday they took me for a run around the old haunts of my ancestors then for tea out. Back home and Mary and Alastair came in for a drink and took photos. Had good supper, looked at other photos, had a good night's sleep. Nice day.

Next day had breakfast and decided this was a nice day for Rousay, the island I was born on. Came over here at 3.00pm today. Booked in at the hotel then went up to Brigend where I was born and took some photos. Met the owners of Westness House, very upmarket, real Upper-class. He was British Ambassador of Sweden, his wife is a titled Swedish lady. He had played polo in India. They invited me in for tea, lovely china brought out. They were very interested in Fiona's career and were happy to have the magazine of Fiona's interview. Met a couple in the hotel from Essex. They also had stayed at the rough farm in Hoy. They had followed me and here we are both, here now in Rousay. I am here until the 5.30pm boat tomorrow night and so are they. Had a meal here tonight – could have been better – did not go into the sitting room after the meal as I found the Englishman a bit overpowering before and during the meal. Just retired to my room.

Had breakfast this morning with the English couple then set off to go round the island, fifteen miles all round with no turn-offs. A lovely day. Stopped and started as I felt like it. Scenery marvellous, the colour of the water and sky wonderful, sometimes almost navy blue/turquoise/pale blue, etc. Saw a two acre plot for sale, £25,000 with Planning Permission for a house. I don't know how that compares with here. Went for something to eat at the restaurant at the pier and who was there before me? The English couple. Met another couple from Penicuik who were involved with East Lothian Pony Club. Crossed back over at 5.30pm but had to get crew chap to reverse my car on again. I tried for B&B when I came off. The hotel looked grubby, tired guest house - owner out. Eventually someone who was back in Finstown phoned someone in Stromness on a farm and I was lucky – two and half hours since I started looking. I booked in for one night, stayed four. I am beginning to tire of going into so many different places. I can leave my bag and toilet bag in same place for a while.

Went to Kirkwall to try and get B&B for a concert I am going to on Saturday night. I tried Kirkwall Hotel where Mum worked but they were full. I got next door, St Ola Hotel, but ate in the Kirkwall Hotel, lovely place overlooking harbour. Went to see Honey (my first cousin) again in Stromness to say goodbye, also Kirsten Harvie who Fiona had sold a horse to. Had a huge farm and had sold twenty seven thousand, three hundred litres of milk that morning. Had coffee with her and her daughter and met her husband who was going off to work at one of their other farms. They are very wealthy farmers, I would say. Went to Sheila Fleet's workshop where her jewellery is made and had a tour, very interesting but all the jewellery is very expensive.

I went to a launderette in Kirkwall on Saturday morning – pouring rain. Got my washing up-to-date. Had tea in Kirkwall Hotel and met another lady who was on a bus tour and was staying at the Hotel. Got a taxi to take me to the concert. It was a wonderful Orkney and Shetland Concert. I really did enjoy it. A taxi back to St Ola where music went on to 1.00am, got to sleep eventually.

Had breakfast in the morning and went to St Magnus Cathedral for morning service where Mum and Dad were married. It was Norwegian day. Went to service led by a Glaswegian minister but as it was Norwegian day, a Norwegian Army Captain in uniform read lessons, one in Norwegian and one in English. Went down to Kirkwall

Hotel and had lunch, then saw the Parade from the harbour at 3.00pm. Kirkwall Pipe Band led it, followed by a contingent from Norway. We, as onlookers, got Norwegian flags to wave to welcome them. Orkney and Norway keep close contact. In 1472, Orkney was given as a Norwegian dowry. The tartan was McKenzie which the Kirkwall Pipers wear.

I then proceeded down to Scapa again to stay for another four nights with Brenda and Morris. I took them out for tea this Sunday. It was a lovely sunny evening. Novelty. I flew to Papa Westray from Kirkwall leaving my car at Brenda's. Morris took me to the plane – Loganir - twelve minute flight. I was petrified - only three of us in it but the maximum is eight. I was sitting directly behind the pilot, propeller going at the side of me and all this water underneath. We were only thousand feet up. I was wanting to hold on to the girl next to me but managed to control myself - the most scared I have ever been in my whole life. I understand the big planes are up about twenty thousand feet – I was scared to look down. When the engine would slow down I thought this is it, we will be in the sea now.

We landed on grass in Papa and cruised onto a small tarmac patch. Jim was waiting to meet me. I was staying overnight with him and his wife Morag, who used to keep their horse at the Riding Centre twenty five years ago, when they lived in North Berwick. Morag had a scone and cup of tea ready.   We spoke for an hour. Jim was away at the one and only shop run by the Islanders but so well stocked. The boat brings the stores twice a week, weather permitting. They have five large deep freezers full. I had a lovely room and a great meal, well presented. I was the only one staying on the Monday. She had been full for three weeks then full again for the rest of the week. Three self-catering people from two cottages came along to join me for the meal. They had been before. Most interesting, a gentleman from America, a Professor of Biology, retired of course, and a retired English couple who had been in the hotel trade but sold out and bought a distillery which their son runs and they are enjoying retirement wherever. We had wine presented at the table. We took photos, told each other our life stories and had a lovely evening. Jim ran them home. Morag does the cooking, Jim waits the table – a great host. He has written twelve books and is working on his thirteenth at the moment. I bought his latest one which he autographed for me and wished me all the best in my writing career which is my next step, I hope. The visitors were quite agog at how much I had done from dairy farming, onwards through vegetable market with 5:00am starts, market research, teaching at private school and local one, starting riding centre after working with horse and gig on beach and post office, charity work at local hospital, secretary at riding school, now bringing me to age seventy seven and retirement at last with no break from leaving school until now.

I had walked down to the pier when I arrived before dinner and saw a lovely refurbished church with doctor's surgery held on Wednesdays and coffee mornings held there also and other meetings. Lovely kitchen and toilets, etc.

After breakfast on Tuesday morning, I was getting the 1:02pm flight back to Kirkwall. I went for a walk on Papa Westray after breakfast and I met the District Nurse on her travels. I asked where Mid House was as I had read Maggie's book in Jim and Morag's house. She is ninety and still drives her Ford Fiesta round the island, goes to

Church, to coffee mornings and the shop. Everyone keeps clear as her eyesight is not good. She farmed her land until she was seventy and her nephew now has the land. The District Nurse, Fiona, an Irish lady said 'jump in. I am going there this morning if you don't mind waiting until I go into the surgery in the Church to check the answer machine' as she is nurse, stand-in doctor and social worker. We arrived at Maggie's sitting by her Rayburn, her box bed beautifully made up. I had a nice chat with her asking her if the tractor always started and she said 'oh, yes but I had a puncture one day and that was a different story'. I saw the children out in the playground, all five of them, only seventy people on the Island altogether. The teacher earns £58,000 a year. How I would have loved that job. Jim gave me a cup of coffee when I got back as I had walked back from Maggie's by the old pier, plenty of time to think. I thought I would call my book The Full Circle as

I was born on Rousay in 1932 and then back the same month in 2009 after retirement. That surely is a full circle.

Jim put me back on the plane and Morris was waiting in the lounge of the airport for me. The girl from RSPB was also on the plane - she had been to Westray but I did not see her until we got off at Kirkwall. I had a short talk with her but could not spend time for a coffee as Morris was there. Got back to Brenda's and booked my passage for 12 o'clock from St Margaret's Hope for Thursday. After having some lunch with them, I lay down as I felt I was still on the plane. I was okay when I got up and had dinner with them. Morris, Brenda, Mary, Alastair and I had a drink and supper at night at Brenda's.

Next day, Wednesday, Brenda and I went to say cheerio to Kathleen. Morris checked my car for oil and water. The car had not used a drop. They had washed the car for me when I was away, so kind. Getting ready now for crossing over tomorrow to Gills Bay at John O'Groats. Sea bands laid out again. Then on to Banff for three nights.

Crossed over. Good crossing then motored to Brora where I found very comfortable B&B, went to an Italian Restaurant for a meal. Now back in a lovely sitting room with wood burning stove, so warm I had to open the sitting room door, although it was raining outside. Nice easy chair with a foot stool and writing up my book, clock ticking away on the wall. I shall leave in the morning for Banff. Arrived at Banff after going down and up Berriedale - some climb. Spent an hour at Nairn harbour – very nice break, had something to eat in the café there. I said I would arrive around 4.00pm which I did. I found the place okay.

The little Micra and I are doing well. Had a nice welcome, a good night's sleep.

Went out for a run with cousin Johnnie and his wife, Lydia, a lovely couple, in Johnnie's Vauxhall Marina, - top of the range, lovely car. We had coffee in a restaurant attached to a country store that sold horse clothing and tack, etc. I paid the bill as they are so kind and won't take anything. Watched TV on Saturday night. Britain's Got Talent, Susan Boyle, excellent singing Memory from Cats. Another good night's sleep.

We debated about church on Sunday but we decided against it. We went for a long walk instead, came back and had lunch. I felt tired so went up and lay on the bed for two hours then sat outside writing my book up. Johnnie cooks on Sundays. He made the evening meal and I enjoyed that, then watched semi-final of Britain's Got Talent. Leaving here tomorrow morning to go farther south. Going to phone Raymond and see him on my way down. It is a year this month since I saw him. Arranged to see them on Wednesday after 1.00pm, have two nights to stay on the way.

Left Banff this morning (Monday) Johnnie saw me out of Banff and on the Aberdeen Road. I motored on, got through Aberdeen reasonably well, but had to watch at all roundabouts to be sure I was on the correct road. It was well signposted. I stopped about one hour from Aberdeen, went off on to a side road and found a wonderful café plus the most unusual Post Office attached to it. The computer and machine for your card was in a cupboard in the kitchen so I had to go into the kitchen where the chef was cooking then wait till she appeared and switched the computer on as she had not used it that morning. We did the card bit and then she disappeared for about five minutes somewhere else to get the money. It proves you can run a post office from anywhere. I got back out on to the A90 and kept going to Dundee and thought I would go in there for two nights. I found that very confusing and seemed to go round in circles. Got around Docks then decided it was not for me. I managed to pick up a sign for the A90 to Perth and made for that and continued on down the road. Went off to one village and found a coaching inn. I did not like the look of it, so rolled down my car window and some women were coming out of the school next door with their children. I asked one person "would you stay in here?" and she said "No". Always ask a local. She told me to go to the next village, Inchture, as it has a lovely hotel. She has meals there. I was very impressed when I arrived there so booked in to the Inchture Hotel for two nights. I walked around the village and spoke to the Post Mistress. The Post Office has been in the same family for a hundred years. The daughter, who has it at the moment, was a receptionist at the Marine Hotel, North Berwick but gave it up two year ago to take over when her mum retired. Had a run around Errol. Nothing in it so back to the hotel for some rest and did some of my photo album. Tidied up and locked car again for last time. Enjoyed every day but now seems the right time to finish up.

I'm seeing Moyra and Raymond in the morning, or rather at 1.00pm. arrived in Perth in the forenoon as I was only twenty minutes from Perth. I had time to spare so I made for the Station Hotel where Duncan and I spent the first night of our Honeymoon. It is now called Quality Hotel. I was reminiscing as I was having my coffee, looking at the stairs we went up fifty five years ago. How happy we both were. I took photographs of the dining room where we had breakfast before the porter carried our cases onto the platform for the Inverness train and saw us off on the Sunday morning to spend the rest of the week. I seem to have done the full circle on this venture from being born to being married to widowed and now retired. After having a bit of difficulty finding Broxmouth roundabout, I finally got to Raymond's, having turned back twice but being on the correct road all the time. Had a nice lunch with them and spent five hours there then decided to come home in the evening when the traffic was not so busy. I came down Glen Devon, sun shining, a lovely run. Stopped in Musselburgh for a Luca's ice cream – can never resist it – on to Longniddry, got bread, milk, butter, etc. Home after a wonderful trip and many memories which will be with me forever. I can always reminisce by reading this and recalling each day of my journey.

Back on 27th May, emptied the car and brushed it all out. Drove it to its usual home in the garage. Well done, true and faithful servant, completing over a thousand miles and still needing no top up of water or oil and never let me down. Up farm roads, on and off boats, round cities and towns with my little Micra and Raymond's detailed route on the passenger seat. A safe and successful journey was complete.

Part Six

Orkney Dream Trip Over

Back now, a retired person in my own home, I could not believe I had the freedom. I felt like a bird out of a cage after thirty two years behind a counter.

The thing I most treasured was that I could get up in the morning when I felt like it – no more clock-watching. I had time to read my paper and have breakfast. Wonderful! It made me realise this is normal for retired people. I have such a beautiful large garden, five lawns actually, plus other areas. I can go out when I want and spend as long as I want, come in and make a cup of tea and go out again. I have a lovely summer house. How blessed, in a complete private area with a huge car park. I have the railway station opposite with a short train journey, approximately twenty five minutes and you are in the centre of Edinburgh.

Still carrying on with my Post Office duties, I have many friends whom I visit and they visit me. I like meeting people. I make conversation easily. I go away for long weekends with my friend Isobel who stays about ten minutes' drive away, also in a small holding. We have had numerous trips to the Borders, Lake District, Pitlochry - a great favourite. Each time I had a Monday holiday, we would have three or four days away. We also spent every second Saturday evening at each other's homes and have a sherry and some supper.

The years move on and we all get older. Some of my friends I have had for over seventy years, one who I started school with, but who, after a seventy three year friendship, sadly has passed away. Another is in the Borders, Kelso actually. We have been close friends since our early teens. I love the trip, driving down to Kelso – the scenery is beautiful. I usually go for lunch with her, she is also widowed, then we chat, have a cup of tea around 3.00pm and then I leave around 4.30pm. I stop at Carfraemill Hotel - very good food. My favourite is their prawn cocktail followed by a wonderful meringue sweet. Then I continue on my way over Soutra Hill with my tapes playing good music all the way and get home around 6.30pm – a wonderful day. We keep in touch by telephone a lot.

Unfortunately, as the years pass on, so do some of your friends. I have some in nursing homes now or are housebound. I never ever forget them. I always keep in touch. I have around eight people on my rota and they always seem to be so pleased to see me and want me back as soon as possible. If I can make part of their day a little different for them, it gives me great satisfaction. For the ones who are housebound, I usually make my basket ready with a flask of tea or coffee, two cups, two plates, two napkins and some nice cakes or biscuits. In that way, I do not want them to make any effort putting on a kettle or wondering if they have any biscuits, etc. I just pull in a chair next to them and say 'sit still! I have all the necessities here. I am here for a chat'. I never phone them, I just arrive - that saves them trying to prepare. If it is summer time, I often just take a carton of Luca's ice cream. I am so glad I am still driving and can move around to see them or take them out for a run in the car if they are able to go for coffee or lunch and, as I move around myself so much, I always have conversation.

I feel totally blessed that I have the health and ability to be independent and just go if I feel like it, also so blessed with a daughter five minutes up the road who can come at short notice. She is so attentive I see her most days even although she is still running her own business equestrian centre. My other daughter has her own show-jumping horse business, competing, buying and selling nationally and internationally. Her horses jump abroad a lot. She does not compete at as high a level as she used to as she is now sixty years old but she schools them on to a certain level and gets a young rider to do the large courses. She gets in touch with me most days and comes down to see me when she can. Her yard is at the foot of the Pentland Hills near the ski slope. She breeds her own stock. I am always fascinated by the new foals and then follow their progress when they go out to compete. My highlight is when Fiona phones me and asks 'are you in today or this evening, I could come down, will Anne be around?'. We get it all arranged - sometimes it is for coffee in the forenoon or it could be lunch or afternoon tea or a meal in the evening. Whenever I know the time I start preparing, setting up the kitchen table, getting everything organised before they arrive as we talk all the time, discussing what each one of us has been doing since we last met. The main subject is always horses which I can relate to with no bother, as I have lived it for many years. I don't feel I am a mother at these times. I feel more like the elder sister. We reminisce, we laugh, sometimes a few tears but that never lasts long. The kettle switched on for another cup of tea and we are laughing again. We never look at the time. There is a clock on the wall where Anne sits, but no one thinks of looking at it. So many plans have been made round the kitchen table. The Orcadians always say the best conversations are made round a table. Suddenly Fiona will glance at the clock and say 'My goodness, I must get up the road to Edinburgh. It is almost midnight'. It sometimes is after that. Anne will say, 'so must I. Raymond, my husband, will be in bed'. I see them off, tell Fiona to phone when she reaches home as I can then relax knowing she is safe. While I await the phone call, I am tidying up, washing dishes, clearing the table, etc, and I'm usually almost ready for bed when the telephone goes. Those are such wonderful times, money cannot buy that. It makes my life so much more interesting. The three of us quite often go out for a meal together. A family is such a blessing. I now have four grandchildren Suzanne, Richard, Stuart and Victoria, and four great grandchildren: Calum, Euan, Sofia and Tom. There are always birthdays, wedding anniversaries, christenings, etc. I am always invited to them all and made to feel so special by them all. Christmas always is a great get-together.

I feel very fortunate at the age of eighty-six to be still driving and have the independence it gives me to just go. I have just changed my car recently, so I am not thinking of stopping yet. I do realise you just take each month, week, or day as they come but I intend to carry on as long as I don't feel I am a danger to anyone. I would not carry on regardless.

I daily give my thanks to God for my health and family and the wonderful full life I have had up to this point.

May at fifteen years old

Duncan and May at a dinner dance in Longniddry

May receiving the Riding for the Disabled Trophy
at Appin

Duncan and May's fortieth Wedding Anniversary

May receiving certificate from Post Office Inspector and customer who wrote the letter

The Drem Post Office Garden in full bloom

East Lothian Courier, September 5, 2008   www.eastlothiancourier.com

AROUND THE COUNTY

Well-deserved long service award for postmistress of thirty years

May the post be with you

by Kirsty Gibbins

AFTER serving her community as postmistress for more than 30 years, Drem grandmother May Fairbairn is looking forward to a well-deserved rest – and her first proper holiday in years!

May, 75, was presented with a long-service award last Tuesday by Post Office representative Alicia Haslam, to mark her years of dedication to Drem's postal services.

"I'm honoured to have received this award in recognition of my 30 years service in Drem Post Office, especially as the branch is under public consultation at the moment," said May, who has two grown-up daughters, Anne and Fiona.

"I have enjoyed serving the community and have always valued my customers and have always found it an effort to greet them with a smile.

"Though I will be staying in Drem when I retire, I think the few customers that I have now will miss me serving them in the post office."

May, whose husband Duncan passed away eight years ago, has lived in Drem since 1954.

Happy holidays

Though fond of the village and its residents, she is looking forward to enjoying a break when she retires from her post in mid-November.

"The first thing I'm definitely going to do is have a long holiday," said May, who also volunteers at Roodlands Hospital in Haddington and helps out at her daughter Anne's Appin Equestrian Centre, Drem.

"I'm originally from the Orkney Islands so I think a nice long stay there would be lovely."

As part of Post Office Ltd's Network Change programme, Drem is one of four county villages that is earmarked to have a reduced postal service installed in mid-November.

A weekly two-hour service is scheduled to commence pending six weeks of public consultation, which began on August 18.

Ms Haslam said: "The service that Mrs Fairbairn has given to the post office for over 30 years is truly outstanding.

"On behalf of Post Office Ltd and all the community, I would like to thank her for all her hard work and effort.

"Despite the fact that we are having to close post offices because of falling customer numbers, it is still important that we recognise the work of individuals."

MAY with her long-service award

East Lothian Courier Article – Long Service Award for thirty years' service for May

May visiting Orkney

Acknowledgements

Peter Kerr, Joan Houston, Louise Amos and Heather To

32148036R00112

Printed in Poland
by Amazon Fulfillment
Poland Sp. z o.o., Wrocław